"Only Nixon"

His Trip to China Revisited and Restudied

James C. Humes
and
Jarvis D. Ryals

Foreword by Edward Nixon

UNIVERSITY PRESS OF AMERICA,® INC.
Lanham • Boulder • New York • Toronto • Plymouth, UK

Copyright © 2009 by
University Press of America,® Inc.
4501 Forbes Boulevard
Suite 200
Lanham, Maryland 20706
UPA Acquisitions Department (301) 459-3366

Estover Road
Plymouth PL6 7PY
United Kingdom

All rights reserved
Printed in the United States of America
British Library Cataloging in Publication Information Available

Library of Congress Control Number: 2009931299

ISBN: 978-0-7618-4738-0

Back cover photo: Professor James Humes, Dr. Jarvis Ryals, Ambassador Ji Chaozhu, and Mr. Edward Nixon.

∞™ The paper used in this publication meets the minimum requirements of American National Standard for Information Sciences—Permanence of Paper for Printed Library Materials, ANSI Z39.48-1992

To the Children of
James Humes and Jarvis Ryals
With the Firm Belief
that They will seek Challenge,
Manifest the Curiosity,
and Widen Their Horizons
in the Spirit of Their Parents:

Mary Humes Quillen
Rachel Bailey Humes
Jennifer Ann Kuchta
Jennifer Ryals Rothstein
Thad Franklin Ryals
Christopher Michael Kuchta
Scott Matthew Ryals
Laura Beth Ryals

"Only Nixon"

"Only Nixon, a Republican president, could have pulled it off."

        Ji Chaozhu
           The Man on Mao's Right
           From Harvard Yard to
           Tiananmen Square, My Life
           Inside China's Foreign Ministry

           Ambassador to the Court of St. James
           Under secretary-general of the United
           Nations for Economic and
           Social Development

Peoples are very much alike
But by practice they become wide apart.

> Confucius

What may be most surprising is how much China and the Chinese people—geopolitics notwithstanding—have in common with the rest of the world.

> Ji Chaozhu
> *The Man on Mao's Right*
> Beijing, 2008

Contents

Foreword		ix
Acknowledgments		xi
1	A Nixon Returns to China in 1998	1
2	Nixon Has Second Thoughts on Chiang Kai-Shek	7
3	Convulsion in China	13
4	Nixon Returns to the World Arena	23
5	Mao: A Lion in Winter	33
6	The Handshake of History	40
7	"Only a Republican President"	54
Bibliography		73
Index		75

Foreword

Edward Nixon

In the wake of my brother's history-making mission to China in 1972, I have made many trips to that nation—mostly to conduct geological studies, mineralogical research, and other non-government related surveys of commercial opportunities in that vast country.

My trip with Professor James C. Humes and Dr. Jarvis D. Ryals in September, 1998, however, was the most insightful and fascinating. Of course, I had heard firsthand from my brother about the behind-the-scenes maneuvering to set up his trip as well as the events that transpired there in February, 1972. And I have been moved to reread the historical accounts published by my brother, Dr. Kissinger, and others.

Yet our trip in 1998 afforded a unique perspective. We were able to see the pioneering trip in 1972 from the Chinese vantage point—an inside view from them regarding those historic events. The Chinese we interviewed were the English-speaking and American specialists in their diplomatic corps who, under Premier Chou En-lai's tutelage, had laid the groundwork for my brother's phenomenal reception. At that time, most of them were just beginning their foreign-service work. Later, in the sunset of their careers, they would be ambassadors in such English-speaking nations as Britain, Canada, Australia, and the Bahamas, or as consul general in a city like Chicago. Yet invariably they would tell us that their finest hour of service was those years of 1971-72 when they helped make history.

As the brother of China's most revered American, it is always an unsettling experience for me to visit the People's Republic. For better or worse, I share my famous relative's looks, including the ski-jump nose. In America, I travel in relative anonymity except when people hear my name and make the immediate association. But as an American in China, people on the street make the connection without even hearing the name. The face of Richard Nixon is perhaps the most recognized of any Caucasian in China. Even children greet me with "Nee-ko-sahn, Mr. Nee-ko-sahn!"

This recognition is a mixed blessing since I am by nature reserved. The spotlight is something I shun like an albino avoids sunlight. Of course, on the trip with Jarvis Ryals and James Humes, I had to assume a frontal role as the late president's brother. But whenever possible, I delegated any occasion for lengthy remarks to James Humes. Jamie, who was a White House speechwriter for several presidents including my brother, is an accomplished wordsmith and no stranger to the podium. A prolific author, as well as a professor, he has addressed audiences in all fifty states and twenty or so foreign countries. The author of *Nixon's Ten Commandments of Statecraft* and a Nixon appointee who served in both the White House and the U.S. State Department, Jamie is as knowledgeable as any on my brother's contemplative manner of thinking. More importantly, he and his wife, who worked for my brother when he was Vice President and President, are longtime Nixon family friends.

Jarvis D. Ryals, M.D., a prominent neurologist and psychiatrist, is another friend I have come to know well, particularly on our trip to China. After each interview, Jarvis, Jamie, and I would share our thoughts and reactions. Jarvis was indispensable on this trip in 1998, because he took careful notes on each of the interviews, which formed much of the basis for this book.

In the three and a half decades since the Nixon visit, historians and political scientists have written twenty or more books on the momentous breakthrough journey that changed the face of geopolitics. *Only Nixon*, however, is unique in its perspective since it affords us an inside look from the viewpoint of the Chinese. In addition, James Humes, who has made more than ten trips to the Richard Nixon Library and Birthplace in Yorba Linda, California, brings intimate knowledge and some hitherto unrevealed insights into the shaping and evolving of my brother's thoughts on China. From his years in Congress, his eight years as Vice President, and particularly the following years out of office when he contemplated another campaign for the presidency, Humes and Ryals show how Nixon planned to make an opening to China the fulcrum in a new kind of balance designed to bring peace and stability to the world.

Acknowledgments

First, we thank our wives, Dianne Humes and Mary Jo Ryals, not only for their advice but for their tolerance of our Saturday luncheon sessions in plotting and revising this book.

Appreciation should also be extended to Samantha Kirk at University Press for her assiduous and meticulous editing.

We are deeply indebted to former President Gerald Ford for his interview with us when he offered his insights into Richard Nixon's global views and diplomatic strategies.

We value the encouragement to write this book from President Nixon's daughter, Julie Nixon Eisenhower.

Winston Churchill II also enhanced the book with his comments to us about his grandfather's esteem of Richard Nixon.

In addition, we continue to be grateful to Father John Taylor and the Richard Nixon Library and Birthplace staff at Yorba Linda, California.

Former British Cabinet Minister Jonathan Aitken, author of NIXON A Life, was helpful.

We also would like to cite the able services of photographer and craftsman Steve Bigley.

As a Schuck Fellow at the University of Colorado at Colorado Springs, I, James Humes, am deeply indebted to Steve Schuck and the Schuck Foundation's president, Don Griffin, for their assistance that enables me to continue my lecturing and scholarly studies.

Chapter One

A Nixon Returns to China in 1998

The late president's brother, Edward Nixon, made a journey to China in 1998. With him were the authors, Professor James C. Humes and Dr. Jarvis D. Ryals. Their purpose was to interview those in the People's Republic—the Chinese Foreign Service elite—who had helped lay the groundwork for President Nixon's historic visit in 1972. The three Americans were surprised by the enthusiastic reception by the Chinese diplomats.

China's respect for the late president's brother was not unexpected. Without the presence of Edward Nixon the invitation would not have been tendered. The trip was the idea of Dr. Jarvis D. Ryals, a Colorado neurologist. He had met Professor Humes when he was a visiting professor at the University of Southern Colorado in Pueblo [now Colorado State University at Pueblo], and who had recently published a book, *Nixon's Ten Commandments of Statecraft* (Scribner, 1997). The work had been triggered by the former president's leaving to that author, at his death, a card listing ten rules in diplomatic negotiations and strategy. That had prompted his editors to explore the book idea of the assessment of Nixon as a world leader by those who knew him best—both in America and abroad. To that end, the authors met and talked to former president Gerald Ford [Professor Humes had assisted Ford in the writing of his memoirs *A Time to Heal*, (Harper & Row, 1979)], former Secretary of State Henry Kissinger, former British Prime Minister Edward Heath, and Member of Parliament Winston Churchill II who gave his grandfather's assessment of his meetings with Nixon when the British Prime Minister met with the then Vice-President several times.

It was the suggestion of Dr. Ryals that they go to China to ascertain the views of those diplomats who had worked with President Nixon, Dr. Henry Kissinger and others in regard to the president's visit in February, 1972—particularly those who were protégés and assistants to Premier Chou

En-lai. James Humes, and his wife Dianne Stuart Humes, had known the Nixon family for many years. Mrs. Humes, who had served abroad in the Foreign Service, had been recruited by Vice-President Nixon for his staff in 1958 from the Eisenhower White House. For Nixon she drafted greetings to conferences, messages for anniversaries of organizations, or letters to heads of state. Professor Humes, while a law student, also worked part time in the Nixon office on research. In the course of those years they would come to know, in addition to the Vice President and his wife, Mr. Nixon's mother, his uncle Ernest Nixon, and the brother Edward Nixon, as well as the Nixon daughters Tricia and Julie.

Later Humes would be, for almost two years, a White House speech writer for President Nixon. He then served in the U.S. Department of State as Director of Policy and Plans. In the same period his wife would again be a chief "message" writer in the Nixon White House.

Edward Nixon, a geologist by profession, had by 1998 already visited the People's Republic on 21 occasions. (Once on their 1998 visit, the Chinese host informed the group "Mr. Nixon probably knows more about Chinese rocks than any Chinese.") Edward Nixon is seventeen years younger than his presidential brother. In looks he is a 6'4" version of his famous sibling. Because he features the same ski-nose mouth and chin of the most recognizable American face in China, he would prompt the delighted cries of "Mr. Nee-ko-sahn, Mr. Nee-ko-sahn" from children in the three cities they visited. Edward idolized his older brother, his mentor who, among other things, paid for his tuition at Duke University. Edward Nixon, by nature shy and reticent, avoided the spotlight in his brother's years as Vice-President and President and was almost embarrassed by the attention lavished on him when we were in China in 1998.

President Nixon may be a controversial figure in American history, but in China he is revered. He is an icon for his bringing the two great nations together in his epic visit in 1972.

Thus his brother Edward would be the catalyst in securing an official invitation for the authors to have the opportunity to learn at first hand the reactions and opinions of key Chinese diplomats to President Nixon.

To that end, the authors went to Seattle, Washington in 1997, to enlist Edward Nixon to be the lead member for the trip. His exploratory letter that emanated from that visit, secured for the three of them a meeting at the People's Republic embassy in Washington D.C. At that time Professor Humes would arrange for the Chinese Ambassador to deliver a later speech to his Philadelphia club, The Union League, at a Foreign Policy Luncheon. At that luncheon there were further discussions about the proposed trip to the People's Republic.

The invitation came from Ambassador Jiang Chengzong, an Executive Council Member of the Chinese People's Institute of Foreign Affairs (CPIFA) headquartered in Beijing. He had been a former Deputy Foreign Secretary and a close associate of Premier Chou En-lai. This delegation of four, that now included Mrs. Humes, left San Francisco for a flight to Beijing on September 20, 1998, arriving the next day. The trip would comprise 11 days. The cities in order of their visit would be Beijing, Hangzhou—the lake resort and favorite retreat of Chairman Mao Tse-tung—and Shanghai. They had VIP treatment, the same level of accommodation as the then former vice-president Dan Quayle, who was visiting at the same time. (Professor Humes, who had visited the People's Republic in 1985 to lecture to several Chinese universities on a tour arranged by the State Department, could note the difference in reception by their Chinese hosts in 1998. This time it was the 'red carpet' treatment.)

Their Chinese host, Ambassador Tang Longbin, an Executive Council Member of the CPIFA that was noted above, had organized the trip this way: In the mornings they would meet one or two of the Chinese diplomats who in 1971 had helped prepare and plan for the Nixon visit. Then in the afternoons, they would replicate the Nixon trip in 1972 by inspecting the same sites of historical interest that the presidential entourage had visited. Those stopping-off places would include, in Beijing for example, the presidential palace where President Nixon met Chairman Mao along with Chou En-lai for discussion, the Forbidden City, the home of the Emperor, as well as the Great Wall and the Ming Tombs some fifty miles outside the capital city.

In Hangzhou the sites for visiting were Chairman Mao's villa (where the Chinese Chairman would vacation to renew himself physically and mentally, and write his 'Mao's Sayings' and poetry there), the nearby lakes, and the site of a redwood tree planting in 1972 by President Nixon. (It was barely surviving by 1998.)

The four also visited in Shanghai the former home of Madame Sun-Yat-Sen, whose husband was the founder of the modern republic that ended the Chinese monarchy on October 10, 1910. (10-10 is a national holiday in both the People's Republic and Taiwan, where Generalissimo Chiang Kai-shek retreated in order to continue his Nationalist government after his defeat in 1949 by the Red Army.) Incidentally, Madame Chiang Kai-shek was the younger sister of Madame Sun-Yat-Sen.[1] They also would plant another American oak tree in the Shanghai Garden where Mrs. Nixon had planted an American seedling in 1972.

A 'photo-op' was arranged on each of these visits with elaborate ceremony. Edward Nixon would stand or sit where the president had and the president of the Institute, Ambassador Jiang Chengzong, would assume the role of Chairman Mao or Premier Chou En-lai. In Shanghai, Dianne Humes would play the part of Mrs. Nixon. Madame Sun-Yat-Sen's house is now an elementary school for gifted children, mostly the offspring of high ranking members of the Communist Party in Shanghai. (Curiously, the American these English-speaking children were most eager to learn details about was Michael Jordan, the basketball star. One student even wore a Michael Jordan sweat shirt.) The young pupils presented a flower arrangement to Mrs. Humes, as their predecessors had to Mrs. Nixon.

Sites like the Great Wall of China are must-see stops for any world traveler but as scholars interested in the Nixon trip, their trip to such sites yielded some revealing insights:

For example, the night before the Nixon entourage was scheduled to visit the Great Wall, five inches of snow fell making the two-lane blacktop road to the Wall impassable. (Nowadays it is a four-lane concrete highway.) No snow removal machines existed then in the People's Republic. The dire situation was reported to Premier Chou En-lai who mobilized 750,000 Chinese to take their household brooms and sweep through the night to remove the snow from the road all the way from Beijing to the Great Wall—the fifty mile distance was approximately 250,000 feet, so each person had only four inches of highway to sweep clean of snow!

Our daily guide during our visit was Ambassador Jiang Chengzong, who might be described as the Chinese version of the American political advance man in 1972. He was the one Chou En-lai dispatched to round up the snow sweepers. Jiang Chengzong was a round-faced, jovial, and enthusiastic host whose informal manner was enhanced by his open collar sport shirt and ever present grin.

Ambassador Tang Longbin had also organized the Nixon trip to the Ming Tombs whose subterranean caverns featured an interred legion of Ming soldiers with their ancient weaponry. In the freezing temperature of that February winter the Nixon entourage witnessed ten pairs of Chinese men in ties and three piece suits playing chess on the tables outside the pavilion that rested above the burial ground. Our guide confided that he, with Red Army officers with rifles backing up his request, had commandeered the men for the staged matches. Some of them, said our guide laughingly, did not even know how to play chess! But it was thought, he explained, that the chess players would enhance the vision of a worker's paradise to the visiting Americans.

A Red Army general at the underground caves had encountered his own problems. Helen Thomas, the UPS reporter covering the Nixon trip, needed to make a phone call back to Washington. The general who was the ranking military officer who was in charge of supervising the caves went to the security gate where there was a telephone but the private on duty there would not yield up the phone to the general. The general was irate. In that time— during Mao's enforced egalitarianism of the Cultural Revolution—officers did not wear their rankings and the lowly private had never met the top general. Thus it was required that the general relay the order to the colonel who passed it on to the captain and then to the private's superior, the sergeant. Helen Thomas would eventually get her phone.

Ambassador Tang Longbin also organized the reception for President Nixon at the Presidential Palace before the meeting with Chairman Mao. Mao's wife, Chiang Ching, was one of the 'Gang of Four' who had militantly opposed the invitation to the capitalist arch-devil. When she learned the Chinese would play the hymn 'America the Beautiful' to greet Nixon on his arrival she unleashed a tirade upon our guide, who was the organizer at that time—"What do you mean 'America the Beautiful'—it should be America the Ugly, America the Hideous, America the Capitalist Exploiter of the Masses." Ambassador Tang Longbin, a young and junior functionary at that time admitted that he feared some measure of disciplinary action or worse from Madame Mao, and in desperation sought the help of Chou En-lai. Chou En-lai then went to her and explained that 'America the Beautiful' referred to "purple mountain majesties" and "fruited plains"—the physical beauty, not the capitalist system. Begrudgingly, Madame Mao relented and the crisis was averted.

Ambassador Tang Longbin also related to us that a principal duty, in Chou En-lai's instructions, was to keep the press corps entertained and distracted. The Chinese had originally balked at Nixon's desire to bring the press to cover the mission. They were used to conducting negotiations in secret and behind closed doors. But 1972 was a presidential election year and Nixon saw the value of such photo-ops featured back in America. Accordingly Nixon took 74 journalists-- mostly from the television world. Nixon originally had planned to bring an entourage of a thousand from the White House, as well as from the State and Defense Departments, but it was negotiated by the Chinese down to 500.

Chou En-lai told Ambassador Tang "Keep them busy with all the sights, full with sumptuous food and happy with lots of drink. And don't forget—have the prettiest young women waiting and in attendance."

We also learned how close the Nixon mission came to being aborted when General Alexander Haig, Kissinger's Deputy in the National Security Council, came over on a planning trip following up on Kissinger's secret visit. A boat trip in Hangzhou had been scheduled by the Chinese. The voyage gave a literal meaning to 'frosty reception' when there was no heat in the boat in the cold lake air. Only tea—without biscuits, much less food—was provided. The Chinese hosts made no attempts at conversation. Only a call to Chou

En-lai saved the day. The mayor of Shanghai, one of the 'Gang of Four' that was angered by the idea of inviting Nixon, had tried to torpedo the pending Nixon visit. Actually a feast had been spread out but the Mayor's minions took it away and turned off the heat. Chou En-lai took it up with Mao and Mao expressed regrets and reprimanded the Shanghai Mayor.[2]

As insightful as these behind-the-scenes anecdotes are in adding color and texture to the Nixon trip, the real surprise of our 1998 visit to China was the eagerness of these diplomats to tell of their role in preparing and planning the visit. One of these Chinese envoys we interviewed was Ambassador Zhang Yijun, who would cap his diplomatic career heading their embassy in Ottawa, Canada. This tallish diplomat, however, considered his most significant service was as a young Foreign Service officer planning the Nixon trip. Ambassador Zhang Yijun said "We were part of one of history's greatest events, and we have been waiting to tell our story and our contributions."

'Interview' in a sense, is the wrong word. Words spilled out of them in pride of what they did. Our questions turned out to be mainly clarifications of what they said.

We came originally to hear how Chinese diplomats assessed Nixon. They had little to say on that except their esteem for the U.S. president was unqualified. They viewed our trip as an opportunity to carry back to America their role in bringing about this diplomatic triumph.

All of our Chinese Foreign Service participants in our meetings were their English speaking elite. Their personal hero was not Mao, but Chou En-lai. He had shielded them from imprisonment or death during the Cultural Revolution. They would eventually rise in the Foreign Service to be Ambassadors to Britain, Australia, Canada, the Bahamas and other English-speaking posts. But their role in preparing for the Nixon visit in the early part of their service they remember as the high point of their careers.

NOTES

1. Nixon, *Leaders*, 243
2. videotape

Chapter Two

Nixon Has Second Thoughts on Chiang Kai-Shek

On December 21, 1959, co-author Humes (hereafter Humes or James Humes), his wife and other Nixon staff were invited to Vice-President Nixon's residence on Forest Lane in the Northwest section of Washington. It was a holiday party.

During the occasion Humes approached Nixon as he sampled a Chinese egg roll. "Someday", Nixon pronounced, "I'm going to China."

"Formosa?" Humes queried. Formosa was the island where Generalissimo Chiang Kai-shek had fled in 1949 after Mao Tse-tung's Red Army drove the Nationalist forces from the mainland. Nixon frowned and said curtly "I said *China*, didn't I?"

"What about Chiang Kai-shek?" Humes asked Nixon.

He answered dismissively "He's a stupid man. The brains are in his wife. He is a small man, only capable of running a small island."

Some months later that desire of Nixon to visit China surfaced publicly. George Dixon, a Washington columnist who had married the daughter of Democratic Senator Denis Chavez of New Mexico, wrote in a column in March, 1960, of Nixon's mentioning such a trip to him in a private conversation at the Nixon's. When a reporter queried President Eisenhower about the article at a press conference, Eisenhower scoffed at the idea as "ridiculous." Dixon, (whose step-daughter was a friend of James Humes), told him later at dinner at their house that Nixon had even made inquiries at the State Department sounding out the possibility.

In 1953, soon after he was sworn in as Vice-President, Nixon had been sent to Taiwan, the capital of Nationalist China on the island that the Japanese called Formosa. In a series of speeches Nixon lauded the Chiang Kai-shek government. The government was so pleased with his series of four speeches that they presented them in a book and distributed it to libraries in America.

Nixon predicted the "Red Rulers on the Mainland" could not last long. "In the end it will be the cause of freedom, the cause of representative government, rather than the cause of slavery and totalitarianism that will triumph in China."

At that time the Nationalist Chinese lobby in Washington was in its heyday. The chief spokesman for its cause was the senior senator from California, William Knowland. Capital reporters often derided him as "the senator from Formosa." In the summer of 1953 Knowland had succeeded the dying Robert Taft as the Senate Republican Minority Leader. But by 1959 Knowland was no longer a political force. He had been defeated by Pat Brown in a race for governor of California.

In December, 1959, Nixon was just about to announce his candidacy for president. He offered as his credentials the best trained and most traveled Vice-President in history. The Vice-Presidency (an office which one Vice-President, Jack Garner under Roosevelt, had called "not worth a bucket of warm spit") had become for the first time the stepping stone to the White House. President Eisenhower in the past eight years had made Nixon a "deputy chief of state" and "deputy party leader." Nixon represented the President in close to a hundred countries, at inaugurals, state funerals and other good will state visits. Only months before, in 1959, Nixon was the first American at the highest level to visit the Soviet Union. (The 'kitchen debate' with Nikita Khrushchev resulted from that trip.) Khrushchev was just one of the many national leaders of whom Nixon had the opportunity to take the measure. Prime Minister Winston Churchill, French President Charles de Gaulle, German Chancellor Konrad Adenauer, Italian Premier Alcide de Gasperi, Ben Gurion of Israel, Ho Chi Minh of North Vietnam, Fidel Castro of Cuba, Prime Minister Robert Menzies of Australia, and Prime Minister Paul Henri-Spaak of Belgium, are just some of heads of government he met and talked with. By December, 1959, Chiang Kai-shek, with whom he had met with several times both in Taipei and Washington, in Nixon's eyes had suffered by comparison to some of those leaders.

Eisenhower had also virtually made Nixon the chief spokesman for the Republican Party. Eisenhower, a career military man, privately despised most politicians and was not comfortable in a partisan role. It was a two-edged sword for Nixon. On the one hand, it solidified his ties with the Republican Party regulars who would choose the presidential nominee in 1960. On the other hand, in the role of the designated party attack man, he would speak for Republican candidates all over the country, and take partisan aim at the Democrats. That would undermine any appeal he might have to independents or Democrats in 1960 whose votes he would need to win as a Republican candidate. The Republicans, after all, were a minority party. Eisenhower had won handsomely because his heroic military popularity in Word War II projected an image above party. If Nixon were to win, he had to appeal to some of those same Democrats and independents who had voted for Eisenhower.

Fred Greenstein, a political science professor at Princeton, wrote *The Hidden Hand Presidency* subtitled *Eisenhower as Leader*. Eisenhower, said Greenstein, made an administrative practice of having 'lightning rods' around to deflect the flak and let him appear as "Mr. Nice Guy" with that smile of his as broad as his native state of Kansas.[1]

Eisenhower's Chief-of-Staff, former Governor Sherman Adams of New Hampshire, was nicknamed "The Abominable 'No' Man." (Yet, Humes' wife at the White House said that the staff was more afraid of Eisenhower himself than the taciturn Adams). The famous Ike smile masked a temper of Eisenhower, which in German means 'hewer of iron'. (When James Humes and his wife first met him in the Oval Office on their first wedding anniversary, he shedded the 'Eisenhower' for the public "Ike," looking like a Norman Rockwell portrait of a sixty-seven year old Huckleberry Finn.)

Secretary of State John Foster ("Brinkmanship") Dulles was his 'lightning rod' in diplomacy. Ezra Taft Benson in the Agricultural Department was another. So was Treasury Secretary George Humphrey ("A depression that will curl your toes.")

In politics, Nixon was Ike's 'lightning rod.' Nixon would deliver a speech to Republican faithful charging Dean Acheson's words that South Korea was not "within our perimeter of defense" were "an invitation to invasion." Eisenhower would smile ruefully and say 'that's Dick for you.' Nixon was selected by Eisenhower to be 'hatchet man' for the Administration. After the re-election of the Eisenhower and Nixon ticket in 1956, Nixon sent a message through others that he would like to beg off from that partisan role in order to burnish his image as a statesman. Adams dismissed the Nixon request.

The increasing respect for Nixon was helped particularly by three incidents—his subdued presiding over the cabinet at the time of President Eisenhower's heart attack in 1955 (compare Secretary of State Haig ("I'm in charge here") at the time when Reagan was shot), his courage in confronting the Communist mob attack in Venezuela in 1958, and his 'kitchen debate' with Khrushchev in 1959.

For that last mission, Soviet Trade Minister Mikoyan had been sent to Washington in 1958 to set up the later visit by Nixon. In their three hour discussion, Mikoyan had let slip some stunning facts about the Soviet Union: numerous grain shortages; difficulties in collectivization; and some Soviet experiments with some profit incentives. Nixon found Mikoyan's unexpected and candid revelations so significant that he asked the interpreter to get the original transcript so that he could then have it translated. In the report he received, all mention of failures, as well as mention of profit incentives, had been deleted. Nixon reported this to Secretary of State Dulles. As Nixon related to James Humes, "Dick," Dulles said, "I know we have communists over here but forget it. It won't help you. I want you to win in '60. The press will destroy you if you bring this up."

James Humes did a paper at Nixon's request in 1959 on the effect the Hiss case had on his career. His analysis stated that it established Nixon as a nation wide figure that led to his Senate victory in 1950, and Eisenhower's selection for him as Vice Presidential candidate two years later. Yet the bringing down of Alger Hiss, so popular with the Eastern Establishment, as a perjurer on his communist affiliation, earned him the unmitigated animus of the Eastern press. Although at the time of the House investigation of Hiss, the *New York Times* commented favorably on Nixon's role and that of William Rogers, the attorney retained by the House Un-American Activities Committee. Nixon would be tarred by the later "anti-anti-communism" mood that became revolted by the antics of Senator Joe McCarthy two years after Hiss. (Rogers would become Nixon's close friend and later his Secretary-of-State.)

Nixon was never close to McCarthy. Privately he believed McCarthyism gave the liberals the tools by which to undermine anti-communism. Actually it was the Kennedys who were close friends of McCarthy. McCarthy arranged for Robert Kennedy to be appointed investigator for the Senate Government Operations Committee. In fact, McCarthy was a godfather for his daughter Kathleen, (later a Lt. Governor of Maryland). Senator John Kennedy in 1955 pointedly did not vote on the Senate censure of the Wisconsin senator—allegedly on the advice of Joe Kennedy, his father and backer of McCarthy.

Liberals persisted after the Hiss conviction to portray Hiss as a victim who would be someday vindicated. Professor Allen Weinstein of Smith College, although originally inclined to sympathize with Hiss, found after study and research that Hiss was indeed a communist. Later the secret Verona files of the U.S.S.R., which were released by Premier Yeltsin in 1996, revealed that Hiss had received payments from the Soviets.

Although a staunch anti-communist, Nixon early began to separate the ideological from the geo-political in his view of the Soviet Union. In January, 1946—two months before Churchill's Iron Curtain Address—Nixon delivered an insightful address to a local service club as a returning naval veteran just before he announced his congressional candidacy. From his studies as a lieutenant commander in service in the Pacific, he came to the conclusion that the history of Russia from the Czars to the Commissars was seamless. Centralized and brutalized tyranny was the pattern from 'Ivan the Terrible' to 'Stalin the Butcher'. The aspirations and ambitions of the Russians remained constant—advance and conquest of the countries that lay to their immediate west.[2]

Later as a freshman congressman in 1947, Nixon wrote the Herter Report that recommended that Republicans support President Truman in his initiatives to contain the spread of communism in Europe. That report, and Nixon's break with the Taft isolationists of the Republican Party, was one reason Eisenhower chose him as vice-presidential candidate (aside from the political and geographical advantages of his youth and California residence).

Already in 1960 Nixon believed that a nation's self interest mattered more in foreign policy than ideology. In 1961, in packing up after his defeat for president, Nixon told James Humes "Look at Stalin in 1939—how the communists made a deal with Hitler. The Russians' longest boundary is with the Chinese, the largest nation in the world. A common ideology cannot paper over their competing interests."

During the 1960 campaign a major issue was the defense of the Quemoy-Matsu Islands just off the coast of Taiwan. The two islands were under constant bombardment from the Red Chinese. In their second debate, Nixon challenged candidate John Kennedy's statement that the islands were not worth defending. Nixon—despite his doubts about Chiang Kai-shek—believed that letting the islands go by default would send a signal of weakness to the world. (Margaret Thatcher made the same argument in resisting the advice to let the Argentineans take the British Falklands.)

Senator Kennedy, defensive on that issue, turned the tables by asking why had the Eisenhower administration allowed the Communists to take over Cuba. Kennedy as president, he promised, would intervene militarily. Nixon and Kennedy, as presidential candidates, had been briefed by the C.I.A. on a contingency plan for invasion. Nixon was embittered by the Kennedy proposal in which he exploited his classified top secret knowledge for political gain. Nixon, who did not want the Cubans to prepare for such an eventuality, was forced to argue that our allies in the Organization of American States would disapprove of any armed intervention. This was the only occasion (in the 1960 campaign) that the *New York Times* took a favorable position on Nixon. Interestingly, this was also the only time Nixon got personally angry at Kennedy. They had been friends in their careers in the House and Senate. Indeed, Senator Kennedy gave Nixon a check made out by his father for Nixon's campaign for the Senate in 1950 against Helen Gahagan Douglas.

Nixon, as outgoing Vice-President, participated in the Inaugural Ceremonies, and he commented to his staff on the Kennedy address right afterwards, "Magnificent sure, but it's the most militant inaugural address ever delivered—'pay any price, bear any burden, meet any hardship, support any friend, oppose any foe to assure the survival and the success of liberty.' And to think, Ted Sorensen (JFK's speechwriter), is a pacifist."

Nixon headed back to California to practice law and prepare for a possible run for governor in 1962 to set him for another presidential try. He had not given up his presidential ambitions by long shot. The Cold War and the strategy to win it was his consuming passion, and the presidency was the only place to accomplish that triumph. He was returning to his roots—the shores of the Pacific in which he had waded as a boy. The foreign policy establishment he had worked with as Vice-President was just about all from the East. Nixon still nurtured his dream to see China at first hand as he did Russia. China had to be a key factor to be considered in policies vis-à-vis the Soviet Union.

NOTES

1. Greenstein, 238, 239
2. Aitken, 119, 120

Chapter Three

Convulsion in China

As the new decade dawned in China, the People's Republic was in convulsion. The seeds of that turmoil had been sown by the self-anointed "Great Father" Mao Tse-tung. Among those sections of society whose lives were upended was the foreign language speaking diplomatic service. Most in their ranks could be easily smeared with a 'bourgeois' label. Indeed, anyone with more than a secondary school education was a potential target at that time of upheaval.

Mao in the 1960's saw himself as the surviving 'true believer' since the death of Stalin. The denunciation of Stalin by Soviet Chairman Nikita Khrushchev in 1957 had triggered the beginnings of estrangement from their 'Big Brother' chief communist ally.[1] The Kremlin in Moscow had been 'the Communist Vatican' for Marxists around the world. And Stalin since the 1920's, until his death in 1953, had been 'the Pope.'

Even if Mao had some political differences with Stalin, he deemed Khrushchev's outburst against Stalin an egregious act of heresy. Mao had identified with Stalin and shared with him a peasant background. Stalin, born in Georgia and Mao in Hunan, grew up far from the cosmopolitan centers of Moscow and Leningrad (St. Petersburg), or Beijing and Shanghai, and both despised the intellectual elites in those metropolises. Both had fathers they hated. It was their mothers who had shaped the formative years of both Stalin and Mao. Stalin had been pushed toward seminary and priesthood and Mao sent to an institute that trained future teachers.

If the peasant Stalin took on a personality cult and developed the paranoid fear of a Russian Czar, so did the peasant Mao become a Chinese 'emperor' in his power and absolutism.[2]

In 1958 Mao Tse-tung announced "The Great Leap Forward." The People's Republic would, at whatever cost, become an industrial nation. Millions of peasants at the point of pistols would be conscripted from their fields and forced to set up small "backyard" iron smelters to produce "steel"—but the product of all this effort proved largely unusable.[3]

If Mao was determined to forge China into an 'Iron Age,' he also wanted to anneal and harden the beliefs of Chinese in the communist dogma. The newly allowed criticism of Stalin in Khrushchev's Soviet Union had convinced Mao of what laxness led to. Accordingly on February 27, 1957, Mao delivered a four hour speech to the Supreme Council. Deceptively, he proclaimed no more "excessive" purges. In this context he cited a Confucian maxim "Let a hundred flowers bloom."[4]

Although it was not understood at the time, Mao was setting a trap. His targets were the educated and intellectuals. As he said later to a few cohorts "How can we catch the snakes if we don't let them out of their dens? We want those bastards to wriggle out and let the colors of their stripes shine in the sun. That way we will catch them."[5]

In June, Mao published a circular. In it he targeted for persecution close to ten per cent of "intellectuals" (about five million)—scientists and technicians would be excepted. Those arrested were labeled 'rightists' and deported to do hard labor in remote areas. This purge also had the effect of silencing those in top authority such as Chou En-lai and others in the top echelons who had such bourgeois background connections as teachers, journalists, or merchants.

By his purges, Mao was portraying himself to those emerging nationalist leaders in the former colonial countries of Africa and Asia as the model for would-be Marxist dictators who presented themselves as leaders of their country's masses. True tribunes of the people, preached Mao, would not yield to the bourgeois inclinations of the western democracies. Mao aspired to be a Stalin-like leader and example for the Third World.

China, like other countries in Asia and Africa, had been exploited by the European invaders. Why should Russia, argued Mao, even if the home of Marx and Lenin, be the paradigm for those countries now eager to cast off their colonial shackles? The Slavs were European. They were white—not yellow or black.

But China—even if a country of a billion—was mostly populated by peasants. Such an undeveloped nation was no shining example for these new nationalist leaders eager to shed their own industrial backwardness.

The Soviet Union, boasting its military might of super bombs as well as the scientific triumph of Sputnik in 1957, was the communist nation these African and Asian countries were looking to, not the People's Republic.

China, however, could not afford to break off from its alliance with the Soviet Union. The Chinese needed their technical know-how as well as the shipment of electronic parts if they were to have nuclear capability. Yet Mao would signal his distancing from the Soviet Union by burnishing his ties with Albania. If it used to be said that "Spain was more Catholic than the Pope," Albania was more "Stalinist" than Stalin. Mao made a point now of cementing his ties with this repressive Balkan nation that had already distanced itself from the rulers of post-Stalin Russia. Another communist Balkan country that the People's Republic cozied up to was Romania, whose relations with the Soviet Union had also cooled.

But China's Great Leap Forward crashed. Mao's dream of making China an industrial nation collapsed. Even worse, Mao had jeopardized his hold as supreme leader as tens of millions of Chinese died of starvation.

Starving Chinese began to eat weeds and bark off trees.[6] Many died from stomach blockage after eating handfuls of dirt. Farmers who 'stole' from their own harvest were executed. Children caught swiping morsels of food had their fingers chopped off. One dissident, Wei Jingsheng, later wrote in the *New York Times* that some villagers were so desperate that they exchanged their babies with neighbors to eat as food.

Jung Chang in her biography/autobiography, *Wild Swans*, told of a peasant overcome by guilt, asking to be punished for killing his own baby and eating it. Hunger had been an uncontrollable force. One husband and wife team kidnapped local children and sold them as "wind-dried" rabbit meat at exorbitant prices. Both the father and the couple noted above were executed.[7]

Mao schemes were intended to increase productivity but the opposite effect occurred. "Collectivization, which Mao thought would infuse the population with a sense of group purpose, instead removed the people's incentive to work the fields. Productivity fell, but bureaucrats responsible for meeting quotas falsely reported an upsurge in output and enthusiasm on the part of the people."[8]

Isolated, Mao dismissed the warnings of advisers and believed the grossly overestimated production numbers by bosses eager to get his attention.[9] He put forth a slogan "Capable women can make a meal without food"—the reversal of a pragmatic ancient Chinese saying "No matter how capable, a woman cannot make a meal without food." [10]

In the presence of such famine, Jung Chang at times would not finish her food and was told by her teacher in boarding nursery, "Think of all the starving children in the capitalist world!"[11]

Eventually the mass starvation would compel Mao to react. The grain harvest of 175 million tons in 1961 was only one-third of the target expected. The failure of Mao's policies now began to be acknowledged in the highest circles. "Top leaders made trips into the countryside to see for themselves how bad things had gotten." "Quietly, heroically (against Mao's policies), reforms were ordered. Peasants were given back small plots of land for their own cultivation, the mass back yard production of steel was halted, and big communal dining halls were dismantled because they were inefficient. A ray of realism managed to break through the dark clouds."[12]

Liu Shaoqi supported by Deng Xiaoping openly challenged Mao's authority. At a '1000 Cadre Conference' in 1962 Mao was privately censured by Liu Shaoqi and probably attacked by Peng Zhen, the Mayor of Beijing, as the deaths mounted to over 30 million.

Mao withdrew to his favorite lake retreat at Hangzhou, and left Liu Shaoqi and Chou En-lai in charge of affairs. In Mao's absence, Chou En-lai negotiated a partial rapprochement with the U.S.S.R., where Khrushchev had been labeling Mao an 'ultra-leftist.'

As the former Deputy Foreign Secretary explained to our group of three in 1998, Mao often repaired to the temperate climes and cool waters of Hangzhou not only for the physical stimulus of daily swimming but, even more importantly, for recharging of his mental batteries.

In the rebuke by his peers for the Great Leap Forward failure, Mao had sustained a body blow to his pride and influence as well as his ego. In Hangzhou he would plot his comeback.

In his life Mao would play two roles: military leader and emperor. In the first he was indomitable, but in the second he never quite overcame his insecurity. In Beijing, the capital, the old peasant could never seem to shake off the feeling of inferiority in terms of sophistication and education. Mao had always distrusted intellectuals.[13] The few who fully sensed his sensitivity about his background, like Chou En-lai, were shrewd enough to avoid confrontation and to maintain a low profile. But the ringleaders who engineered Mao's recent slide from supreme authority such as Liu Shaoqi and Deng Xiaoping had set themselves up for later payback.

At this vulnerable time in Mao's life, his new wife Chiang Ching solidified her hold on Mao. She fed both his personality cult and paranoia. She listened to his poems and encouraged him to promote his sayings.

In his reflections at Hangzhou, Mao came to believe that China needed a re-kindling of revolutionary zeal. It was that fervor that inspired his Red Army followers in the 'heroic' Long March in 1935, the 6000 mile slog from Jiangxi to Shaanxi. Communism was their religion and the words of Marx their gospel. But the illiterate peasants who answered Mao's call then were animated by hatred—hatred against the rich, and the mercantile exploitation by warlords, and colonial occupiers.

In planning his comeback Mao would re-ignite the flames of class hatred. In July, 1962, Mao returned unannounced to Beijing. Finding support from Defense Minister Lin Biao, he at once set about reclaiming lost ground with a new campaign against 'rightist revisionists.' In September he used his platform to emphasize the value of "class struggle" and to identify "ideological enemies." Some ministers loyal to Liu Shaoqi were purged.

The next year Mao's vendetta against "the Liu Shaoqi clique" gathered steam. Mao launched a Socialist Education campaign. Work teams were dispatched from cities to the countryside to root out 'local corruption' (i.e. rightists) who were then shipped to work in the fields where their manual labor would then re-instill in them true socialist values.[14]

These teen age recruits charged with rooting out 'rightists' would carry with them the Little Red Book—a collection of Mao's sayings. Later these zealous and violent youths would be called the "Red Guards."[15]

By 1963 Chiang Ching had surfaced publicly as Mao's new wife. The two welcomed visiting President Sukarno of Indonesia that year. Chiang Ching, or Madame Mao, as the new Minister of Culture, endeavored to launch a Cultural Rectification campaign but she was blocked by Peng Zhen, the mayor of Beijing, and Liu Shaoqi's ally.

For the next three years the new 'Mandarins' of China would combat Mao for power and the control of the Party. If the Beijing bureaucrats had the edge in the infighting, the People's Liberation Army (P.L.A.) captains in the countryside were Mao's weapons for winning over the masses. The P.L.A. had sworn their fealty to the supreme commander they had fought under. Liu Shaoqi had maneuvered in vain to keep the army separate from the government, but the Army was carrying Mao's message against "the Rightists."[16]

On May 16, 1966, Mao, with the urging of his wife, launched the start of the Cultural Revolution with a broadside to the Central Committee. At the same time a student group, who took the name Red Guards, staged a protest in Qinghua University against rightist teachers criticizing Mao. Student abuse of their teachers went beyond their tirades in classes. Some were kicked and beaten to death. Mao proudly took note of the Red Guard's violence for two months from his resort at Hangzhou, and turned a deaf ear to Liu's pleas to return to Beijing in order to lend his voice to quell the crisis.

When the three of us in Hangzhou, some three decades later, listened to our group organizers explain in stark understatement the onset of the Cultural Revolution and the overzealousness of the Red Guards in implementing it, we had to read between the lines to understand the full impact.

Ed Nixon, Dr. Ryals, and Professor Humes afterwards tried to imagine if something like it happened in the United States. It would be as if the President in Washington had urged high school students all across the United States to put on arm bands and accost, badger, and harass citizens on the street and in their homes even on invented suspicions and then storm city halls. Such a thing could never happen in America. If they tried it, they would be arrested by nightfall.[17]

Chapter Three

As John King Fairbank and Merle Goldman wrote in their book *China: A New History*, "In the United States the semi-autonomous sectors of a civil society—the professions, business, labor, the church, the media and so on—cannot easily be dragooned."[18]

Mao had in fact set a quota for his Anti-Rightist campaign. Five per cent of those who were classified in their identity documents as 'educated' would be targeted for persecution and be assigned to manual labor in remote places. The term 'educated' meant those teaching in state schools, vocational institutes, and universities. But it also included accountants, bookkeepers, journalists, municipal civil servants, and linguists. Only engineers and scientists, even if they had studied abroad, escaped persecution. Mao needed their expertise.

The label 'rightist' easily stuck to those who had the advantages of advanced education, especially if there had been a merchant or landlord in their family background. And those in lower strata of society were only too ready to hang the dreaded subversive label on the elite. In the late 40's and 50's, when Mao proselytized the masses in his Marxist cause, he had made class revenge his weapon. People were indoctrinated to look up to workers and peasants as the real 'nobles' of life and despise the landlords, merchants, and manufacturers as 'lowly' and 'base.'

In the Cultural Revolution Mao would once again play the 'class card.'[19] Except this time 'intellectual' would be tainted with the stigma once reserved for landlords and merchants. Academics had been among the first to embrace Marxism and support Mao in his fight against Chiang Kai-shek and his Nationalist regime. For these leftists to be labeled 'rightists' was for them a wrenching if not traumatic experience.

Some of these academics had friends and colleagues who had been hunted down and executed in the 1930's by Chiang Kai-shek's purges. Yet Mao would put to death a hundred times more than Chiang Kai-shek.

The foreign and civil service elite, with whom we interviewed on the 1998 trip, admitted to have been stunned and staggered by their being singled out. They had thought it could not happen to them because they were devoted members of the Communist Party. Memberships—open only to the few—were a badge earned by their specialist professional education and training to serve the Party and country.

'Revolution' is a word often devalued by its over-use. But its literal meaning is 'turning' over. Topsy-turvy certainly describes the effects of the Cultural Revolution when bus drivers were appointed to head colleges and university presidents demoted to being janitors in hospitals or mental institutions. (This was the actual experience of James Humes' study-mate, a former university president, at the Center for International Scholars at the Smithsonian in Washington when he was a Woodrow Wilson Fellow in 1982.)

Mao had thrown a match into the smoldering rage of masses of peasants and workers against the educated elite. Such resentment is not confined to China. About the same time as the Cultural Revolution in China, Alabama Governor George Wallace was inveighing against "pointy-head intellectuals" in New York and Washington.[20] A year later, President Nixon mined a similar vein of resentment against the Ivy League and the national media in his 'silent majority' speech in November, 1969.[21]

Yet nothing can be truly compared to the cauldron of society upheaval ordered by Mao at this time. Political rhetoric is one thing—revolution is another. In all history never has such mass political cataclysm been orchestrated from the top. Stalin killed millions in mass purges of his suspected enemies, but in China many were peasants who had only resisted the agricultural collectivization that removed farmers from their ancient fields.

Chairman Mao's aim transcended the usual dictator's elimination of enemies or suspected enemies. He was engineering a radical make-over of Chinese social structure. Devoted Marxists and obedient followers of the Party line could not expect exemption from the new purges. Only engineers and scientists were left alone. But not doctors. The elite of Chinese medical professors, most of whom had received their advanced learning and specialist training in America or Europe, were removed from hospitals. Four decades later hospitals in China are still suffering from shortages of doctors.

One of the former Foreign Service diplomats we talked with was Ambassador Ji Chaozhu. He had a close relationship with Premier Chou, and related his own personal experience with the medical upheaval. When his father, a well known and respected scholar and personal friend of Chou En-lai, became ill, his family knew he would not survive if they took him to the hospital, because farmers had been put in charge there and the doctors had been assigned to manual labor in the fields. A revolutionary from the Translation Department at the Ministry, with no medical training, boasted to Ambassador Ji that he had operated on a patient, and that it was "so simple and easy." So the family kept his father at home and cared for him until he died. Even both the son's and the father's connection to Premier Chou could not save the situation. Ambassador Ji relates this incident in his 2008 book *The Man on Mao's Right*.[22]

Teachers, hospital administrators, bureaucrats, and factory managers if they had a taint of bourgeois in their background were fair game. Only one who had worked as a peasant in the field or who had toiled as a laborer in a factory in Mao's mind-set could manifest the true revolutionary spirit and make the Marxist dream a reality.

Early in the Cultural Revolution Mao's nephew, Mao Yuanxin, had "discovered" that Mao's Little Red Book, rather than medical treatment, was the cure for mental patients![23]

To understand the Cultural Revolution in American terms it is as if a *New York Times* reporter would be sent to work on a wheat farm in Nebraska, or a Yale professor dispatched to Detroit to toil on an automobile assembly line, or the head of the Chinese desk in Washington's State Department reassigned to be an orderly in an Oklahoma hospital. Those uprooted tried to console themselves that their punishment was a fate that was not worse than death.

During this Cultural Revolution one foreign service official, in answer to our questions, would nod 'yes' that their fellow members of the diplomatic elite owed their survival to Chou En-lai.

Still our Chinese hosts resisted talking about their own personal cases of persecution and punishment. They switched the subject when asked. One might compare it to a rape victim. The one violated psychologically frequently feels irrationally a scintilla of guilt. The one raped might look back and question her clothes or conduct. In the same way these who had been targeted for manual labor in remote areas might wonder if they might have entertained in their own mind 'rightist' thoughts. At any rate to talk about their harassment to strangers would be to revisit this period of ignominy and shame.

Even though our Chinese diplomats would not recount their ordeal in being purged and punished, one account may give light to what happened in thousands and thousands of cases. The writer Jung Chang was a daughter of a respected cultural minister in Sichuan, a province in west central China. Her father had joined the Communist Party at age 17 in 1938, at a time when Chiang Kai-shek was arresting known Communists. The writer's father had graduated from the Academy at Marxist Lenin Studies and later engaged to teach semi-literate peasants-turned officials. Later he joined Mao's Army to fight Chiang Kai-shek and as a colonel in Mao's Army, he had married a student revolutionary leader, Jung Chang's mother.

Yet in 1967, when the Red Guards came to Director Chang's cultural office in Chengdu, the capital of Sichuan, they beat him to a pulp and he was sent to work in an agricultural collective in Miyi.[24] Jung Chang, who had become a Red Guard, was devastated. Her mother attempted to assure a future for her children, saying "she did not want her children to be 'black.'"[25] In other words 'second class citizens,' in the categories of "red," "black," and "gray" created by the Red Guards. The "blacks" were the children of landlords, rich peasants, and rightists and were considered inferior to the "reds"—the children of workers, peasants, and revolutionary officials, officers, and martyrs.[26] Interestingly, Chou En-lai, who had been acquainted with Director Chang and respected his work, could not rescue him from the assigned work in a rural collective where diet deprivations and harsh labor would end his life. He died at age 54.[27] Jung Chang recalls at that time she never lost faith in Mao but blamed his wife for the Cultural Revolution.

The position held by Director Chang was different from the ones held by those in the Chinese diplomatic service, but the humiliation, deprivation, and 're-education' punishment was much the same. Director Chang was honest and outspoken on things that he saw wrong in the Cultural Revolution—which lead to his persecution.[28] He told his wife, Jung Chang's mother, "I don't understand the Cultural Revolution. But I am certain that what is happening is terribly wrong."[29]

One who ended his diplomatic career as Consul General in Bermuda was sent to work as a coal miner in Hunan, hundreds of miles from Beijing.

Another, who would cap his stint in diplomacy by becoming Ambassador to New Zealand, had been assigned in the Cultural Revolution to work in a cement factory in Nanking.

Our organizer, Ambassador Tang Longbin, who has been previously described as the 'advance man' for President Nixon's trip in 1972, was the only one who talked more openly of his experience. He became a brick layer and he pointed out to the three of us the row of bricks that he laid in the wall approaching the Forbidden City, the ancient imperial palace in Beijing.

Our daily guide, Ambassador Jiang Chengzong, would also proudly point out the very column on the front of the Great Hall of the People that he helped build.

Without exception, all of our interviewees admired former President Nixon. As one said in a toast, "He built the bridge across the Pacific to the People's Republic."

But their appreciation for Nixon's statesmanship might have been colored by the indirect role Nixon played in saving these diplomat's lives. The Nixon visit in 1972 demanded their English expertise. One by one they were called by Chou En-lai, who was intricately involved in the arrangement of the meeting that was being secretly negotiated.

One of our interviewees was Mme. Zhang Ying, a former Deputy Director General of Information. A petite woman of less than one hundred pounds, wearing slacks, she had spent her diplomatic career attending and organizing conferences in countries including English-Speaking ones in the Third World—Africa and India promoting the party line. Upon her arrest by a Red Guard she was taken from Beijing to work on a tea plantation. For three years she had picked leaves from four foot long trees in Foochow, in Fukien province that borders the Formosa Strait. She had wasted away to 80 pounds before she was called back to Beijing.

She did not hide her debt to Nixon. The head of the 'capitalist dog nation' had been the catalyst that turned her life around—from possible death to a new diplomatic career.

NOTES

1. Fairbank, 385
2. Ibid., 384
3. Ibid., 371
4. Ibid., 364
5. Chang, *Wild Swans,* 212
6. Ibid., 236
7. Ibid., 234
8. Chaozhu, 181
9. Ibid.
10. Chang, *Wild Swans* 223
11. Ibid., 246
12. Chaozhu 202
13. Chang, *Wild Swans* 213
14. Fairbank, 376
15. Ibid., 392
16. Ibid., 387, 388
17. Ibid., 383
18. Ibid.
19. Ibid., 386
20. Aitken, 360
21. Ibid., 389
22. Chaozhu, 230, 231
23. Chang, *Wild Swans,* 477
24. Ibid., 379
25. Ibid., 334
26. Ibid., 294
27. Ibid., 479
28. Ibid., 331
29. Ibid., 297

Chapter Four

Nixon Returns to the World Arena

In 1967, when the People's Republic of China under Chairman Mao in his Cultural Revolution witnessed millions being purged, imprisoned, or executed in a mass oppression that rivaled the worst in Hitler's Nazi Germany or Stalinist Russia, Richard Nixon published an article saying that the U.S. "cannot afford to leave China forever outside the family of nations."[1]

In the spring of 1967, when Nixon wrote these words in an article for *Foreign Affairs* (to be published that fall), the former Vice-President had maneuvered himself into being the front-runner for the Republican presidential nomination in 1968. His political comeback from his defeat for governor of California in 1962, was unprecedented in American history. A tired and testy Nixon in a press conference after the defeat had asserted "You [in the press] won't have Dick Nixon to kick around anymore."[2] A couple of days later, ABC featured a television analysis with Alger Hiss as one of the guest commentators entitled "The Political Obituary of Richard Nixon."[3]

Professor Humes talked with Nixon in June, 1962, as the former Vice-President was preparing to run for Governor. It was in the Wanamaker's department store in Philadelphia where Nixon was autographing copies of his newly released memoir *Six Crises*. Humes, who had just won the primary for Republican legislator against a ten year incumbent, asked Nixon to sign some fifteen books for key supporters. Nixon said that he would have someone package them and send them off to him, and then talked about his campaign. He said that General Eisenhower urged him to run. Eisenhower, he explained, was worried about the surge of Goldwater's popularity in the party and that he also had little regard for Governor Rockefeller after his attacks on his administration's 'missile gap' in 1960.

Then he said "But Jamie, I'm not going to run in 1964 for president. Kennedy will win again and I'll just be like another Adlai Stevenson, a sacrificial lamb in a second losing race. I'm pledging in my governor's campaign not to run for president in 1964—but to finish my term."

What he did not tell Humes was that his wife, Pat, had strongly opposed his decision to run for governor. So did Bob Finch, his former chief of staff as Vice-President. It was not that Nixon could not win, but rather if he did win, the challenges presented to him in Sacramento were not the issues that really engaged his mind. The Cold War—not the community college system in California—was what he talked about with his friends. Even if California's budget in spending was larger than all but seven nations in the world, matters of budgets, revenues and taxes were subjects that did not fascinate the former Vice-President.

In 1960, Nixon was the first (and only) Vice-President to have gone to all fifty states, but the 1962 campaign for the suburban sprawl California was more difficult. For one thing, he had to experience an unexpected tough primary fight because the John Birch Society-backed Joe Schell challenged him from the right. If Nixon manifested political courage in lashing out hard at "the radical fringe right," it was not sound political judgment. (Reagan would refrain from such charges when he would run and win in 1966.) Barry Goldwater with his best selling *Conscience of a Conservative* was winning followers in southern California, and these 'true believers' saw Nixon as emblematic of Eisenhower's moderate Republicanism which they despised.

Although Nixon won the primary handily, he alienated some Republicans that he needed on his side if he was to beat the incumbent Governor Pat Brown in a state where Democrats outnumbered Republicans. Nixon, embittered by his defeat, let loose his frustrations at the end of his gubernatorial public career at his famous press conference, noted earlier.

California was a dead end for Nixon, so he moved to New York to become the lead name partner in a major city law firm, now named Nixon, Mudge, Stern, Baldwin, and Todd. If the state of Governor Nelson Rockefeller afforded no political base, it did give him a perch in the international business center of the world.

By bringing some major accounts to the new Nixon, at the Mudge firm he consolidated his new position. Shortly thereafter, he took his wife and two daughters for the first real extended holiday trip to Europe. But Nixon's idea of vacation was to re-establish his contacts with European leaders and statesmen. On a six week tour he had meetings with Generalissimo Francisco Franco of Spain in Barcelona, British Foreign Secretary Lord Alexander Douglas Home in London, the German Foreign Minister Willy Brandt in Bonn, Italy's Defense Minister Giulio Andreotti in Rome, and Egypt's President Gamal Nasser in Cairo.[4]

The highlight of the trip was a private luncheon with President deGaulle. Pointedly, the U.S. Embassies did not afford the traditional courtesies to the former Vice-President as well as former presidential candidate as was routinely done for other former national candidates or high office holders in the past. The Eisenhower administration, for example, had instructed the State Department to set up meetings in foreign capitals for former Democratic candidate Adlai Stevenson. Nixon made the calls to various leaders on his own without any color of official sanction. In Paris, deGaulle read about Nixon's visit in the newspaper and invited him to be his special guest.

At the beginning of the lunch, Nixon delivered a toast in French without notes ending with words from Rousseau to describe the leadership gifts of his host, "He thinks like a philosopher but governs like a king."[5]

President deGaulle, in turn, in English noted that Nixon's career, like his own, had suffered its own setbacks which only made him stronger and ended his toast by predicting that Nixon would come back to head his country.[6]

Nixon was moved to tears and deGaulle would ever remain a special hero in his life. (In Nixon's final speech a week before his death in 1994, he would cite deGaulle's quotation from Sophocles when he retired from the French presidency, "Only when you have seen the sunset does the sunrise seem so glorious.")

President deGaulle had this advice for Nixon when he returned to high office, "Well, what are you Americans going to do? Are you going to break down the Berlin Wall? If you are not ready to make war, make peace, but make it on a very strong basis, from strength rather than weakness."[7] In their discussion, Nixon heard for the first time the word 'détente'. 'Entente' he knew but détente's meaning 'the lessening of tensions' was a new diplomatic term as well as strategy.[8]

Diplomatic strength even more than military capability could be the key to 'détente'. That could be achieved, suggested deGaulle, by negotiating with China now instead of waiting too long when America would be forced to deal with them in the future when they would have consolidated their status as a world power.[9]

In later years, after he left the White House, Nixon would describe the evolving foreign policy initiative that was shaping up in his mind. "The Chinese Game made the Russian Game work, and the Russian Game made the Chinese Game work."[10]

Nixon was taken by the mystique of deGaulle. No book in Nixon's extended library had more notes penned on its page's margins than deGaulle's autobiography *The Edge of the Sword*. One underlined passage was: "Great men of action have always been of the meditative type. They have without exception possessed to a very high degree the faculty of withdrawing into themselves."[11]

Along with deGaulle, Nixon's favorite political heroes were Winston Churchill and American presidents Woodrow Wilson and Theodore Roosevelt, all of whom were in his words "men of thought as well as action."[12] "Kennedy," Nixon told James Humes, "lacked the substance to go with his considerable style."

No doubt, Nixon's opinion of JFK was shaped by his years of association with him. They both were naval veterans elected to Congress in 1946. They served together on House Committees. (Once they even shared a sleeping train compartment in a ride to McKeesport, Pennsylvania, near Pittsburgh, in 1947 where they would debate the Taft-Hartley Labor Relations law.)

In 1995, James Humes was a dinner guest of former Florida Senator George Smathers, at the Metropolitan Club in Washington. Smathers was a good friend of both men. He had been an usher at Kennedy's wedding, and introduced Nixon to the Cuban-born Bebe Rebozo, who in presidential years would frequently host Nixon in Key Biscayne, Florida. He related to Humes how he and Kennedy would play on Nixon's lack of a sense of humor: "Kennedy would tell a nonsensical story and then laugh uproariously. Nixon would join in, thinking it had some sexual reference and he didn't dare risk asking the point."

"Yet," said Smathers, "If Kennedy thought Nixon was a bit 'nerdish,' he respected him. Old Sam Rayburn (the Speaker of the House) told us freshmen congressmen in 1947 'there are show horses, and work horses.' Well, Nixon was the work horse—unlike Jack and me, he always did his homework and wrote the committee reports. We did the partying and then signed on to the report Nixon drafted later."

Nixon was in a New York taxi cab, just returning from Dallas where he was doing some legal work for Pepsi-Cola, when he learned of the Kennedy assassination.[13] He immediately penned a handwritten note to Jacqueline Kennedy and received one in return: "I know how you must feel—so long on the path, so closely missing the greatest prize—and now for you, all the questions come up again—and you must commit you and your family's hopes and efforts again . . ."[14]

Like looking through a kaleidoscope when a spin shifts all the pieces into a completely different picture, the presidential scene had radically changed. Lyndon Johnson, although an able and seasoned politician, was not the popular and charismatic personality that Kennedy was.

As the presidential election years of 1964 loomed, Senator Barry Goldwater was more than a candidate, he was a 'movement'. Governor Rockefeller was leading the moderate Republican forces against the conservative hero. Nixon figured he might just emerge as a compromise candidate at the San Francisco convention the following July.

Professor Humes, a Pennsylvania state legislator at that time, was committed to Pennsylvania Governor William Scranton who had been urged to run by General Eisenhower, but then later asserted his neutrality. Humes with some other state legislators went to Gettysburg to press the General to back Scranton, in April, 1964. Eisenhower told them that Goldwater already had enough delegates to win the nomination: "Nothing that I could do can change it. My brother Milton, and my son John, are working for Governor Scranton. That shows my personal inclination. I have to stay neutral to have some influence on him [Goldwater] after he is nominated."

If Rockefeller ever had a possibility of winning, it was to defeat Goldwater in the California primary in June. The governor's sudden announcement that he was divorcing his wife to marry Happy Murphy shattered those chances. Conservative Republicans in 1964 still had significant prejudice against divorce.

Humes saw Nixon in San Francisco: "All buttoned up, aren't you?"— Nixon was frowning, referring to his 'Scranton for President' pin.

At the convention Nixon introduced Goldwater:

Now I present to you the man who has carried, and proudly carries, the title of Mr. Conservative. He is the man, who by the action of this convention, is now Mr. Republican. And he is the man, who after the greatest campaign in history, will be Mr. President—Barry Goldwater.[15]

Humes, in a Governor Scranton staff suite, watched on television as Nixon received a fifteen minute standing ovation in the Cow Palace.

Then when Goldwater followed in his address to say: "Extremism in the defense of liberty is no vice. Moderation in the pursuit of peace is no virtue."[16] the author was shattered. He knew Goldwater would be defeated for the election in a Democratic landslide in November because he had now given LBJ the chance to tag him with the "extremist' label.[17] In addition, Goldwater rejected a willing Bill Scranton as a VP choice to bind up party wounds, and chose Congressman Bill Miller instead—a mediocrity who brought nothing to the ticket but the rant of attack rhetoric.

But in the certain defeat of Goldwater, Nixon returned to the national party scene. Governor Rockefeller, however, refused to support the convention choice. His sulking in Albany would severely hobble his chances for the Republican nomination in 1968. Many Republican congressional candidates, such as the future president George H.W. Bush, wary of too close association with Goldwater, asked Nixon to speak in their districts.

Taking five weeks' leave from his law practice, Nixon campaigned vigorously for the Republican cause, making over 150 speeches in thirty-six states. In a conversation with Bob Finch, he compared his effort to joining the doomed army of Napoleon on the retreat from Moscow.[18]

In the electoral catastrophe that followed, the Republican Party was in dire need of a political Phoenix who could rise from the ashes and heal the wounds of a party fractured between its liberal and conservative wings. Nixon sought that role. In retrospect, he regarded his decision to campaign for Goldwater in 1964 as the single most important step that he took on his return to power during the wilderness years.[19]

In early December, 1965, James Humes and his wife visited Charles K. McWhorter in his Greenwich Village apartment. McWhorter, now a lawyer with A.T. and T., had been a former national chairman of Young Republicans. He had joined Nixon's Vice-Presidential staff in 1957. McWhorter had just sent out his Christmas cards, each with short notes, to more than 6000 Republicans from lists which he had amassed in his Young Republican years.

Charlie told them that Nixon had asked him to make a list of all those Republican congressmen who had lost by close margins in the Johnson landslide. Nixon remembered that in 1938 Republicans picked up scores of seats—many of which had been lost in FDR's 48 state sweep of Governor Alf Landon in 1936.

In the Nixon, Mudge office, Nixon, McWhorter, and a young partner Tom Evans had worked out a plan for the 1966 election. Nixon would spearhead a campaign to win back these marginal seats, and so position himself to make a run for the presidency in 1968.[20]

Two weeks before the election, Nixon, who had earlier only attacked President Johnson on domestic policy issues, hit him hard on his announced plan to withdraw U.S. troops from Vietnam if the Northern Vietnam Army would withdraw theirs. Nixon spotted the flaw: The Vietcong inside South Vietnam would be allowed to continue the war even if the North Vietnam troops withdrew.[21] "Is this a quest for peace or votes?" Nixon derisively asked.[22]

Johnson exploded at a White House press conference. "I don't want to get into a debate . . . with a chronic campaigner like Mr. Nixon," and went on to savage the former Vice-President in personal terms.[23]

"Nixon," Humes was told later by Charlie McWhorter, "was ecstatic." LBJ had put Nixon back in center stage as the national spokesman for the Party.[24] The Republican National Committee provided him a half hour of prime television time to answer the president.[25] At the end of his talk, which was a series of questions on his Vietnam policy, Nixon added this deft dig, "I respect you for the great energies you devote to your office, and my respect has not changed because of the personal attack you made on me. You see, I think I can understand how a man can be very, very tired and how his temper can then be very short."[26]

In the election two days later, the Republicans scored a resounding victory by picking up forty-seven congressional seats, three senate seats, eight governorships, and 540 seats in state legislatures. Forty-four of the sixty-six House candidates for whom Nixon had spoken were victorious. He had been elevated from 'chronic campaigner' to the 'Leader of the Opposition.'[27]

Nixon then did an astonishing thing. On "Meet the Press" in January, 1967, Nixon announced he was starting a six month moratorium on politics. He had once told staff members in 1959, that "campaigning is a matter of rhythm and timing". Against all advice and to the surprise of the media, Nixon did not try to capitalize on the comeback victory of Republicans.[28]

As he told his biographer, Jonathan Aitken (later a Minister of Defense in Prime Minister John Major's government), "The next six months became one of the most creative periods of my entire life, because it was then I began to see what had to be done with the Soviets and China."[29]

The appointment schedule in his European tour was like a Who's Who in International Diplomacy: former Conservative Party Prime Ministers Harold Macmillan, and Alec Douglas-Home, as well as the current Labor Party Prime Minister Harold Wilson in London; former Chancellor Konrad Adenauer, and current Chancellor Kurt Kiesinger, and Foreign Minister Willy Brandt in Germany; Pope Paul VI, Prime Minister Moro and Foreign Minister Fanfani in Italy; President deGaulle, and Foreign Minister Couve de Murville in France; Prime Minister Paul Henri Spaak and the Secretary General of NATO in Belgium.[30]

After touring Eastern Europe and the Soviet Union (where Leonid Brezhnev alone of world leaders refused his American visitor an appointment) he returned to his law office in New York.[31] After a week he went on a long swing to Asia, and then in April, a five nation tour of Latin America. In June, he was off to Africa and then later to the Middle East.[32]

The Eastern Establishment ridiculed these trips as global showboating to refurbish his political image back home. A *New York Times* columnist James Reston asked, "Is he trying to prove that the road to the White House runs through all the capitals of the world?" . . . "Few candidates have ever seen so many new things and had as little new to say about them."[33]

The esteem and respect of the statesmen and diplomats outside America at that time was a contrast to that of the press and journalist elite in America. Macmillan's former Foreign Secretary Selwyn Lloyd said to his then aide Jonathan Aitken, "Nixon is a brilliant strategist, not a Cold War hack."[34]

Selwyn Lloyd's successor in the British Foreign Office, Lord Home, told James Humes at a dinner in the House of Lords in January, 1990, of his conversations with Nixon. Home was a hard line anti-Soviet. (As Prime Minister Heath's Foreign Secretary in 1970, he sent packing all the Soviet and Eastern European agents and operatives acting under diplomatic cover.) Home said

Nixon was "the most far thinking and strategic planner of any of the world players in diplomacy" at that time.

Former Congressman Robert Ellsworth, who traveled with Nixon to Europe, told Professor Humes later that same year in a breakfast at the Brook Club in New York, "Nixon was often thinking two or three moves ahead—even a generation ahead—He had come to the belief that Europe had become rigid and bi-polar in their thinking. Looking backward I believe that was where the insertion of China into this bi-polar world began to occur to him."

When Nixon returned, he began to work on the article on China for the October, 1967, issue of *Foreign Affairs*, "Asia after Viet Nam." In it he said, "Any American policy towards Asia must come urgently to grips with the reality of China . . . that does not mean rushing to grant recognition to Peking . . . but we simply cannot afford to have China outside the family of nations, to nurture its fantasies, cherish its hate, and threaten its neighbor. There is no place on this small planet for a billion of its potentially most able people to live in angry isolation."[35]

This is in line with the thinking of Britain, who had recognized Red China years before. Co-author Ryals, when an undergraduate between 1957 and 1961, attended a lecture by former Prime Minister Clement Atlee, who was on a lecture tour of the United States. When taking questions at the end of his talk, he was asked why Britain recognized Red China in 1949. His answer was simple and short—"We do not think that eight hundred million people can be ignored."

In his conversations with leaders like Prime Minister Lester Pearson of Canada, Lee Kwan Yew of Singapore, Prime Minister Eisaku Sato of Japan, President Ayub Khan of Pakistan, Prime Minister Robert Menzies of Australia, as well as President deGaulle of France, Nixon sounded out these leaders in follow-up telephone calls that summer and fall.

James Humes remembers when he and his wife visited Nixon's office in early 1968. His wife was an old friend of Rosemary Woods, Nixon's secretary from Congressional and Vice-Presidential days. While the two were reminiscing, Humes flipped through the rolodex on Nixon's desk, and saw these and other names and their phone numbers.

It was then that Humes was introduced for the first time to Nixon's young partner, Tom Evans (a classmate of his brother at Williams College), and Ray Price, the cerebral writer from the *Herald Tribune* who had helped Nixon write the China article.

Humes asked Evans about the potential Rockefeller candidacy that was looming in March. (Rockefeller, however, did not enter that primary, but he had the entire political establishment from Governor Ray Shafer and Senator Hugh Scott in Humes's home state of Pennsylvania behind him.)

Evans answered, "The Boss says that the only 'R' that could defeat him in Miami is Reagan, not Rockefeller." This surprised Professor Humes and would have amazed the mainstream media, who were echoing the line that only Rockefeller could win in the fall, not "the two time loser Nixon." Reagan, even if a growing darling of the right, was at best only a favorite son candidate from California ostensibly to hold the delegation together but not a true candidate.

Nixon, however, cut off any potential attempt by the conservative favorite Reagan by lining up Senators Barry Goldwater and Strom Thurmond behind him.

The death of Robert Kennedy in June, followed by the violent convention of Chicago where Humphrey backed by President Johnson barely beat back the peace wing of the Democratic Party, seemed to give Nixon the edge in the fall: "The candidate," proclaimed Nixon, "who cannot unite his own party cannot be expected to unite his country."

Nixon spoke of a new route to "honorable peace" in Vietnam which would "end the war and win the peace in the Pacific." The Press falsely reported he had spoken of "a secret plan" to end the war. The adjective came from a questioner in the audience, and was mistakenly attributed to Nixon and put out on the UPI wires. The Democrats, and later historians, accused Nixon of concealment and political gimmickry, and only later after his critics enjoyed a field day was the mistake eventually acknowledged.[36] Nixon's plan was to de-Americanize the Vietnam conflict and to start bringing U.S. troops home, which he would announce in the Guam Doctrine of July, 1969.[37]

Nixon's edge in his race against Vice-President Humphrey would disappear in the closing weeks of the campaign. On October 31, President Johnson went on television to announce a breakthrough on Vietnam, saying North Vietnam had agreed to peace talks with all parties—to respect the neutrality of the Demilitarized Zone, and to stop attacking South Vietnam cities in return for an end to the bombing north of the DMZ.[38] Humphrey now surged ahead after this 'October surprise.'[39]

But Nixon did not believe that President Thieu of South Vietnam had been included in this agreement, and he concluded that Thieu would not come to the diplomatic talks in Paris. So Nixon raised questions about it. His judgment was proved correct. On Saturday, November 2, Thieu said he would not participate in the talks.[40] The peace euphoria collapsed, and in the aftermath of collapsed hopes, Nixon would regain his lead to win by 1%—a 43 to 42% majority of 603,000 votes.[41] Nixon was now to be the leader of the world's most powerful democracy.

NOTES

1. Nixon, *Foreign Affairs*, October, 1967.
2. Aitken, 305
3. Ibid., 306
4. Ibid., 318
5. Ibid.
6. Ibid., 319
7. Ibid., 318, 319
8. Ibid., 318
9. Ibid.
10. videotape
11. Aitken, 337
12. Ibid.
13. Ibid., 316
14. Ibid., 317
15. Ibid., 321
16. Ibid.
17. Ibid.
18. Ibid., 322
19. Ibid.
20. Ibid., 323
21. Ibid., 324, 325
22. Ibid., 325
23. Ibid.
24. Ibid.
25. Ibid.
26. Ibid., 326
27. Ibid.
28. Ibid., 327
29. Ibid.
30. Ibid., 327, 328
31. Ibid., 328
32. Ibid.
33. Ibid.
34. Ibid., 329
35. Ibid.
36. Ibid., 352
37. Nixon, *RN*, 394, 395
38. Aitken, 363
39. Ibid.
40. Ibid., 364
41. Ibid., 367

Photo 1. Beijing. Diaoyutai State Guest House. Left to right: Ambassador Jiang Chengzong, Mrs. Dianne Humes, Chinese interpretor Miss Tang RongRong from Anhui Province, Mr. Edward Nixon, Professor James C. Humes, and Dr. Jarvis D. Ryals.

Photo 2. Beijing. Diaoyutai State Guest House. Jarvis Ryals, Ed Nixon shaking hands with Ambassador Jiang Chengzong, James Humes, and Dianne Humes.

Photo 3. Beijing. Diaoyutai State Guest House. Dianne Humes, James Humes, Ed Nixon, Miss Tang RongRong, Ambassador Jiang Chengzong, and Jarvis Ryals.

Photo 4. Beijing. Diaoyutai State Guest House. Ed Nixon pointing out a feature of the large painting to James Humes, Dianne Humes, and Jarvis Ryals.

Photo 5. Beijing. China World Hotel. Where the American group stayed in Beijing.

Photo 6. Beijing, China World Hotel. Ed Nixon, James Humes, and Dianne Humes standing by a carved elephant in the lobby of the hotel.

Photo 7. Beijing. China World Hotel. View of downtown Beijing from window of the hotel.

Photo 8. Beijing. Familiar logos.

Photo 9. Beijing. Small boy wearing a Chicago Bulls shirt.

Photo 10. Beijing. Street scene.

Photo 11. Beijing. Ambassador Guo Jiading at left with the group.

Photo 12. Beijing. Mr. Qian Dayong, second on left, with the group.

Photo 13.   Beijing. On the steps of the Great Hall of the People.

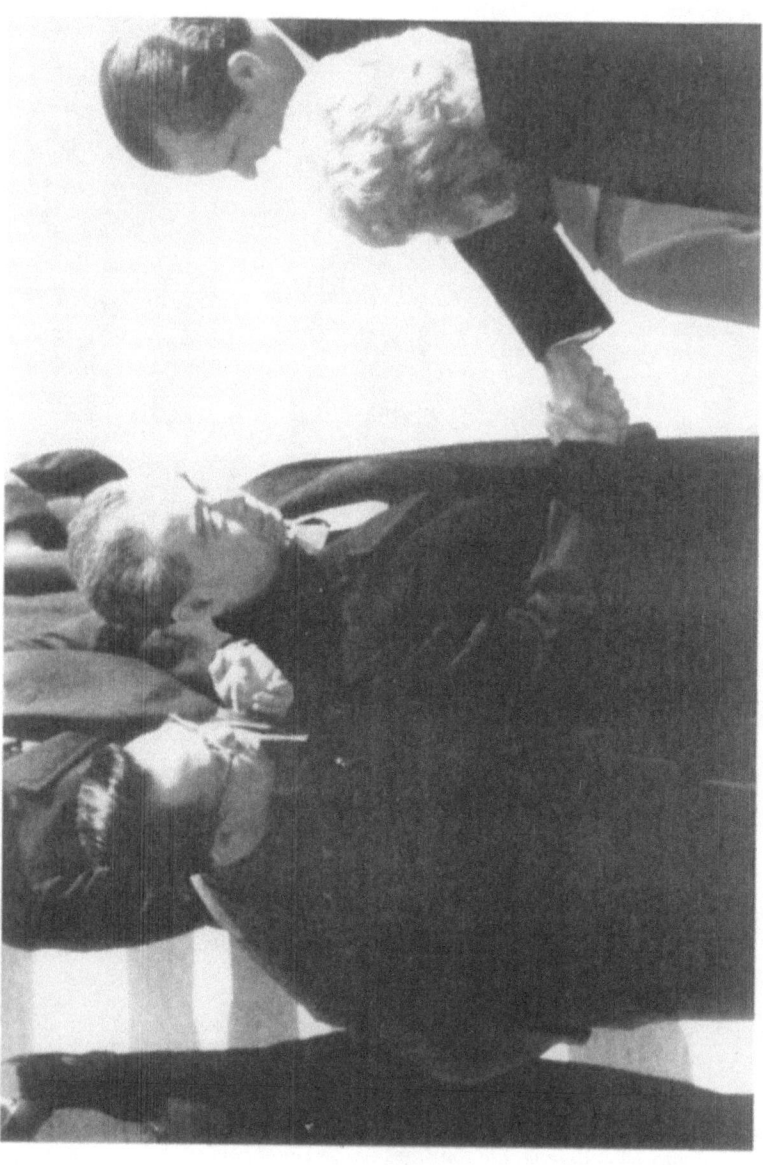

Photo 14. Beijing. February 21, 1972. "The Handshake that Shook the World"—President Richard Nixon and Premier Chou En-lai. The interpreter, Ji Chaozhu, is standing behind Premier Chou.

Photo 15. Beijing. James Humes, Jarvis Ryals, Ambassador Ji Chaozhu *(interpreter on President Nixon's first visit to China in February, 1972)* and Mr. Edward Nixon.

Photo 16. Beijing. Ed Nixon, Mr. Wang Li, James Humes, Dianne Humes, Jarvis Ryals, and Ambassador Jiang Chengzong.

Photo 17. Beijing. Ambassador Jiang Chengzong, James Humes, Dianne Humes, Jarvis Ryals, Mme. Zi Zhongyun and Ed Nixon.

Photo 18. Beijing. Ambassador Zhang Yijun (center) with the group.

Photo 19. Beijing. Foreign Ministry. Vice Foreign Minister Yang Jiechi (center), with the group. By 2008 Yang Jiechi was Foreign Minister.

Photo 20. Beijing. The group in front of the Foreign Ministry.

Photo 21. Beijing. Ambassador Tang Longbin—seated between Jarvis Ryals and Ed Nixon.

Photo 22. Beijing. Lobby of the China World Hotel. Mme. Zhang Ying (third from left) with the group.

Photo 23. Beijing. Tiananmen Square.

Photo 24. Beijing. Forbidden City, the group.

Photo 25. Badaling. The group at the Badaling entrance to the Great Wall, near Beijing.

Photo 26. Badaling. The group on the Great Wall.

Photo 27. Badaling. Ed Nixon on the Great Wall.

Photo 28. Badaling. The Great Wall.

Photo 29. Ed Nixon by a carved elephant statue at the Sacred Way on the road to the Ming Tombs.

Photo 30. Hangzhou. The lake resort and favorite retreat of Chairman Mao Tse-tung. The Chairman's villa.

Photo 31. Hangzhou. The group ready for a boat trip on the lake.

Photo 32. Hangzhou. Ed Nixon in front of the Red Fir tree, planted by President Richard Nixon on the first visit in Feb., 1972. On the left, our interpretor in Hangzhou, Miss Dai Hong "Tracy," talking with Dianne Humes.

Photo 33. Hangzhou. Marker at the Red Fir tree.

Photo 34. Shanghai. Ed Nixon signing guest book at a girl's school.

Photo 35. Shanghai. Ed Nixon greeted by a student with flowers.

Photo 36. Pueblo, Colorado. Colorado State University-Pueblo, March 11, 2005. James Humes, Winston Churchill II, Jarvis Ryals, and Dianne Humes.

Photo 37. Rancho Mirage, California. March 31, 2000. James Humes, President Gerald Ford, Jarvis Ryals, at President Ford's Home.

Photo 38. Lionville, Pennsylvania. Vicker's Tavern, August 16, 2000. Jarvis Ryals, Julie Nixon Eisenhower, James Humes, and Dianne Humes. Vicker's Tavern was owned by an ancestor of President Richard Nixon.

Chapter Five

Mao: A Lion in Winter

While Nixon was making his way back to the world stage, Mao was finding his authority as a global figure of influence diminishing. In 1968, Mao had lived three quarters of a century. Physically for a man of his age he was still fit (two years later he would swim in a cold mountain lake for an hour), yet politically his power had become feckless and flaccid.

If the seventh decade is a time when many individuals might start thinking about afterlife, committed Marxists like Mao ponder their after-death mark on history. The recent years had witnessed little to brighten Mao's page in history books.

The Cultural Revolution was a catastrophe of epic scale. Mao had the vision of reshaping China into a truly classless society where the ultimate evaluation and advancement of every peasant, worker, soldier, teacher, or administrator would be based on one's living manifestation and representation of proletarian ideals.[1]

Mao worried about the People's Republic, with its division of the 'Mandarins' and the Masses—the bureaucratic echelon of the elite at the top and the millions of peasants and workers on the bottom. It was shaping up as not that much different from the China of the pre-revolutionary days.[2]

His Cultural Revolution policies to conscript peasants for the factories, and consign teachers to the fields, lowered the productivity of both. The notion of demoting heads of institutions and hospitals to sanitation work and putting janitors in their place to implant the mind-set of the peasant worker was quixotic, if not idiotic. It may not have hurt the cleanliness of streets but it stunted a student's future and endangered patient's lives.

In an account of the revolution published in Hong Kong in 1986, two Chinese political scientists write:

> For China, the Cultural Revolution remains a colossal catastrophe in which human rights, democratic ideals, the rule of law and even civilization itself was unprecedentedly trampled. Not only was the president, Liu Shaoqi persecuted to death, but tens of millions of innocent people were attacked, abused, or executed.

The Cultural Revolution failed, just as the Great Leap Forward had a decade before. In 1958, Mao had launched an industrialization campaign designed to turn China from a "third world" nation into a modern economic superpower.[3]

In 1957, Mao had boasted to Communist leaders in Moscow that China would overtake America in steel production in ten years. Steel mills and related industries like coal mines were ordered to go flat out to speed up production. Peasants were taken out of the fields to augment the worker force in mines and factories.

Peasants left in the collectivized communes were ordered to set up 'backyard' blast furnaces to bolster steel production (with the result that labor was diverted from the fields and grain yields plummeted).[4] At least 90 million people were forced to construct such home furnaces. They produced not steel, but, at best, pig iron. To feed these furnaces the people were compelled to give up every piece of metal they had—farm tools, water wagons, cooking pots and pans.[5] The regime slogan was: "To hand in one pick axe is to wipe out an imperialist, and to hide one nail is to hide one counter-revolutionary."

Specifically Mao wanted the steel production to make China an armed superpower with might of military machines to reinforce its masses of troops. By 1958, the number of large-arms-centered industrial projects had reached a staggering 1,639, yet only 28 had been completed and they were hardly producing anything at all. Many factories were never completed because of the lack of basic materials like steel, cement, and coal, — and electricity as well. It was said that "Mao was the only ruler in history to produce a rust bowl at the start of industrialization, rather than at its end."

What fueled Mao's accelerated push for steel production was the need for tanks and planes to check the Soviet Union's menacing build-up on their northern border. In response, China mounted an effort to build tank manufacturing and assembly plants. Six factories, at the cost of an equivalent of 3.5 billion U.S. dollars, were erected. Yet these plants were only able to build six tanks a year, according to *Chinese* (2000) by Jaspar Becker.

On August 13, 1969, the Russians crossed the Kazakhstan—the Xinjuang border with hundreds of tanks. Mao had no real defense against Soviet tanks if they chose to move south to Beijing. He had always relied on the massive size of China and its billion population as insurance against invasion.

Mao also feared the Soviets might make a nuclear strike against his atomic installations. In Beijing he had built an underground complex of nuclear shelters.

In June, 1972, in Moscow Professor Humes and his wife were taken to lunch by Victor Louis, to a Ukrainian restaurant. Humes had just left the State Department and a mutual friend, Sir John Wedgwood (of the pottery family) suggested they should meet him. Wedgwood told them Louis was a 'shadowy figure' often used for contacts with the west—negotiating book contracts (such as one for Stalin's daughter) and other deals. Louis gave them as his address a P.O. Box in Helsinki. Louis, who was U.S.S.R.'s first emissary to Chiang Kai-shek in Taiwan, told them the Kremlin had been considering, in 1970, bombing Mao's nuclear test site and deposing Mao for "an alternative leader." (Louis also tried to sell Humes and his wife icons from the Russian Orthodox cathedrals.)

Soviet Chairman Leonid Brezhnev regarded Mao's attempt to set himself up as the true ideological inheritor of the Leninist-Stalinist mantle, particularly to the Third World of Asia and Africa, insulting if not invasive. Diplomatic relations with Beijing had almost been completely severed as Mao endeavored, in the wake of his first hydrogen bomb test in June, 1967, to project himself as the "Great Leader of World Revolution." To spread Maoism across the globe he had set up secret training camps in China with language instruction and the use of arms and explosives.

These insurrectionist mobs, trained by China, attacked the Soviet embassies in Indonesia, India, and Burma. By the end of September, 1967, China had antagonized almost 50 nations with whom it had diplomatic relations. Some of them closed their embassies in Beijing. To mend fences and reposition himself as the Marxist patriarch of the non-Caucasian peoples, Mao tried to have a Third World Conference in Indonesia, which would be presided over by the People's Republic. Little interest had forced cancellation of the proposed Jakarta conference.

In forcing many third world countries to take sides with China over Russia, these countries chose the Soviet Union, which was the other "Super Power" besides the United States, and a potential source of much economic assistance to them.

Mao's insistence that radical and revolutionary leaders sign up with him against Russia cost him particularly in Latin America. Castro, who never visited China during Mao's lifetime, described Mao once, in one four letter word, as a "sh__." There would be no influential Maoist parties in Latin

America in his lifetime. (After his death, a radical group in Peru, however, would adopt his name.)

Even Vietnam answered to the Soviet Union and yielded to their influence and domination. First, Ho Chi Minh had always resented China's historical treatment of Vietnam as a vassal state—as China had traditionally considered the small South Asian countries of Burma, Thailand, Cambodia, and Laos. Second, it was the Soviet Union which was providing North Vietnam with the tanks and weaponry. The Soviet Union saw militarized communist Vietnam not just as an ideological ally, but a geo-political check on China in South Asia.

Mao looked upon the Vietnam conflict with mixed feelings. On the one hand, it delighted him to witness the destruction of the "Yankee imperialist" troops he had once fought in Korea. Yet the possibility of a victorious Vietnam becoming a Soviet satellite to its south was a distinct prospect and a dangerous one.

In March, 1970, Professor Humes, then still in the State Department visited on vacation his cousin Ambassador John P. Humes in Vienna. John Humes was the host envoy for the S.A.L.T. (Strategic Arms Limitation Treaty) talks. The U.S.A., Britain, France, and Italy were on one side, and the Soviet Union on the other. (Humes recalls that the British envoy set off the alarms in the third floor 'chicken coop,' where the allies plotted their strategies. The Englishman had to strip. An electronic device—'bug'—was found, which had been planted in the sole of his shoe.)

One night Humes and his wife were accosted by members of the People's Republic Embassy at the DreiHussaren Hotel in Vienna. For an hour the Chinese harangued them that the U.S., in these S.A.L.T. talks, should never trust the Soviets. To the Humes surprise, they never once mentioned the conflict in Vietnam. When Professor Humes brought it up, the senior member of the Chinese delegation only shrugged dismissively. Their principal bone of contention with the United States was Taiwan, not Vietnam. The depth of Mao's commitment to North Vietnam's struggle against the imperialist and capitalist America might be measured by the discards and often defective weaponry given to their Communist ally—particularly when compared to those sent by the Russians.

At a time when Russia was menacing China's northern border, the People's Republic had a need for allies but its feckless diplomacy had won few friends. The Soviet Union was not only threatening externally, but internally too.

The 'alternative leadership' the Soviet operative and fixer Victor Louis had alluded to was Lin Biao, the number two man in the People's Republic. The son of a textile manufacturer, Lin Biao had entered a military academy and had distinguished himself both in the Long March and against the Japanese.

He then had ingratiated himself with Mao by making the People's Liberation Army the military "missionaries" in the Cultural Revolution. The 'bible' these soldiers all carried was Mao's *Little Red Book*. The loyal Lin also provided Mao the military teeth he needed to purge the Party and reconstruct the party regime.

As a reward Mao rewrote the Party Charter to make Lin Biao number two in the Party and country.

A purblind Lin Biao failed to apprehend fully the paranoia of Mao. He did not fathom the vulnerability such advancement exposed him to. Unlike a Chou En-lai, Lin Biao, as well as his ambitious wife, did not keep a low profile. He also did not discourage a mini-cult celebrating him and drawing to him a new legion of followers.

Lin Biao was hardly the charismatic figure to threaten a Mao. He was a skinny little man in a society where portly was the image of the powerful and weight a sign of greatness. In addition, Lin Biao had all the dynamism and authority of a bookkeeper. Still, insecurity dwells in fears, not facts, and Mao felt threatened by this former soldier he had raised to the highest echelon. For not the first time in history, a leader became jealous of the attention given to a creature of his own making.

What gnawed in Mao's gut was Lin Biao's apparent grip on the army, and its potential for pulling off a coup d'état. If Lin Biao thought that his 'more Marxist than Mao' posture and pronouncements were the way to insure his succession to Mao, he miscalculated. It only enhanced the Chairman's jealousy of him.

By 1971, Lin Biao's actions in portraying himself as China's most dedicated Communist and most implacable opponent of capitalism and the nation that embodied it, made Mao edgy. Mao, at that time, was considering some response to hints from President Nixon to establish better relations as a counter-weight to the Soviet Union.

Lin Biao was not happy when he heard of such rumblings. Furthermore, the one-time general believed that unnecessarily aggravating their powerful Soviet neighbor was risky business. He knew that the Soviet army could easily cut through Chinese defenses faster than Nazi tanks rolled through Poland.

Mao's personal fight with Lin Biao surfaced over a seemingly harmless dispute about the presidency. Chairman Mao wanted the position eliminated. Lin argued that the post (last occupied by Liu Shaoqi) should continue with Chairman Mao assuming the additional title and his becoming Vice-President. Most in the top echelon sided with Lin Biao. Mao was infuriated.

Mao asked Lin to deliver a self-criticism to the top leaders of the Party. Lin balked at this humiliating ritual, even though realizing that his refusal would make Mao an avowed enemy. Lin Biao realized his future in China was over.

He had to cut and run, particularly when his son without his knowledge, had been implicated in a plan to assassinate Mao.

On September 13, 1971, Lin Biao tried to fly to Moscow. His pilot had become aware of Mao's orders to down his plane. Accordingly, the plane flew low to escape detecting radar, but the low flying used up more gasoline than planned. When the plane ran out of fuel, it crashed in Mongolia, killing all nine people on board.[6]

In the past year, Lin Biao had added up the signals correctly to piece together evidence of Mao's willingness to entertain overtures from the United States. Biao was not the only one in the highest echelon of the Chinese party structure to regard this as apostasy. The so called 'Gang of Four,' that included Mao's estranged wife Chiang Ching and the mayor of Shanghai, were also implacably opposed and they were throwing every roadblock they could against any sort of accommodation with, in Chiang Ching's words, "the running dog of capitalism." Mao made efforts to restrain the four plotters, but they were too powerful to discipline. Certainly he could not have his own wife jailed. It would have resulted in too much of a scandal for him.

But in Lin Biao's case, Mao had no doubt had him and his family targeted to be executed as "counter-revolutionaries." That was why Lin Biao was running for his life. Mao would have had him and his family executed without any compunction or a moment's hesitation.

Mao's role model was Joseph Stalin, and his estrangement from the Soviet Union began with Khrushchev's savage denunciation of the Red Leader. Stalin had millions executed in purges of the 1930's, and Mao would surpass Stalin in the numbers of "counter-revolutionaries" slain.

Interestingly, the leader Stalin most respected was Adolph Hitler. It is not as odd as it might seem on the surface for Communist Stalin to admire the Nazi Hitler. Both were ruthless totalitarians. Winston Churchill predicted in the 1920's that the Soviet Union would make a rapprochement with Germany long before it came to pass in 1939, in the Molotov-Ribbentrop pact. At that time Churchill took issue with the conventional wisdom that the two ideologies, Communism and National Socialism, were opposites. Churchill saw it rather in a circle—where 2 degrees East was very close to 178 degrees West. In 1939 Stalin sacrificed ideology for national self-interest in reaching an accord with Nazi Germany.

Three decades later Mao would emulate the pragmatism of his hero Stalin. He would also put the geo-political strategy over ideological solidarity. The first priority was to contain the threat of its giant neighbor: Communism would yield to opportunism.

Zhang Hanzhi, one of the main interpreters for Mao and Chou En-lai, related in the PBS American Experience program *Nixon's China Game* that during the months prior to extending the invitation to President Nixon to visit China, Mao was preparing his associates for the shift in policy toward the U.S. She said that Mao kept telling them "You should know now that our major threat is from the Soviet Union, so this is why we want to break the ice with the U.S. Otherwise, China would face enemies on both fronts."[7]

At age 78, Mao knew his life was soon coming to an end. He had witnessed his failed efforts to rival and overtake the Soviet Union as the Communist leader to look up to for the Third World. The People's Republic was more isolated than ever, and Mao knew his first priority was to safeguard its future. To that end, the cornered Mao was ready to entertain accommodation with his ideological enemy—Capitalist America.

Gao Wenqian, the former official biographer of Chou En-lai at the Chinese Communist Party Central Research Office for Documentation, says in his 2007 book *Zhou Enlai: The Last Perfect Revolutionary* that Mao had once been heard to murmur to himself "China and the USSR are at war. It is up to the United States to make the next move."[8]

Wenqian then goes on to say of Mao, "He would 'use the barbarians to keep down the barbarians,' the ancient strategy of Chinese rulers. As the Grand Strategist, Mao, the master, would open up relations with the United States to deal with the USSR."[9] Later Wenqian stated "The invitation to Nixon was an obvious diplomatic triumph."[10]

Wenqian was able to write such a definitive uncensored book about Chou only after he left China. When the book was first published in Hong Kong in 2003, it was immediately banned in the People's Republic.[11]

NOTES

1. Fairbank, 383-387
2. Ibid., 384
3. Ibid., 401-405
4. Ibid., 371
5. Chaozhu, 182
6. Fairbank, 401
7. videotape
8. Wenqian, 6
9. Ibid.
10. Ibid., 232
11. Ibid., cover

Chapter Six

The Handshake of History

While the Chinese coterie led by "the Gang of Four" plotted to derail any accessibility granted by Chairman Mao and Chou En-lai to the United States, so in America the State Department was stonewalling any initiative by President Nixon to open up a dialogue with the People's Republic.

Henry Kissinger would jokingly complain to Chou En-lai in 1971 while preparing for the Nixon mission: "Our State Department is pro-Soviet." In the sense that the Foreign Service careerists were more interested in arranging some sort of détente with the Soviet Union, than with China, it was true. Few old China hands remained in the State Department in the early '70s. Chinese speaking experts such as John Service had left with the taint of being pro-Mao and anti-Chiang Kai-shek.

On the other hand there were many careerists who had served either in the Soviet Union or other Slavic countries in Eastern Europe. Familiarity breeds favoritism, or at least a bias.

Compare the situation with the Middle East when President Truman in 1948, against the advice of the State Department, recognized Israel. The experts on the Middle East were all 'Arabists,' with knowledge of Arabic and the experience of postings in Cairo, Damascus and other capitals. There were no Zionists in the State Department. (Secretary of State George Marshall would quietly resign in protest to the Truman decision on Israel and Dean Acheson would succeed him.)

Presidents like Truman and Nixon soon realized when they headed the Executive Branch, including the State Department, that it was the career bureaucrats that shape most of the Departmental policy. In most cases, the Cabinet Secretaries are manipulated by the staff over which they preside.

In the State Department 'going native' means when the Ambassador to a foreign country begins to reflect and recommend the policies of the host country instead of the interests of the United States. In the same way, politically appointed Secretaries become advocates for the policies of the career bureaucrats who serve under them. It is different in corporate America where a new C.E.O. can enforce a change in the attitudes and priorities of personnel.

The State Department under Richard Nixon (Professor Humes served there briefly as a political appointee) consisted of mostly Democrats, at least in their party of registration. Although they were not partisan in their politics, their top political hero—if pressed—might have been Adlai Stevenson. Their first priority is their career and advancement in the Foreign Service. Because of that, "C.Y.A." (Cover Your Ass) guides any implementation of policy. That passive approach mitigates against boldness in favor of consensus.

Nixon's first choice for Secretary of State was Thomas E. Dewey, the twice nominated and twice defeated Republican presidential candidate. Dewey declined and recommended Bill Rogers, the one time Dewey protégé who became Attorney General in the second term of President Eisenhower. Rogers had been a close friend, and perhaps his closest advisor in the 1960 campaign. When Nixon protested that Rogers knew little about foreign policy, Dewey replied "He doesn't need to. He is an old friend of yours, you can trust him, and he's a top lawyer who has handled international clients. Anyway, you will be your own Secretary of State."

But an influential or great Secretary of State, like Dean Acheson or John Foster Dulles, enters the office with knowledge of foreign policy and his own set of priorities. Rogers had neither of these and so was amenable to the diplomatic careerists in the State Department. That meant adherence to the status quo and resistance to change.

When Nixon took office in 1969, there had been ongoing talks between the People's Republic and the United States taking place. Altogether 135 meetings in Warsaw had taken place since 1962; the new president directed that these meetings continue even though they had become a charade. The two sides met across a table and repeated their scripted demands without any real discussion. Basically they wanted the U.S. to end support of Taiwan and the U.S. did not.

Nixon asked the U.S. Ambassador, Walter Stoessel, to signal to the Chinese representative that this new administration was entertaining a new shift in its policy on China, and that he was to convey that message personally. The rigid format at the talks, argued the State Department, did not lend itself to such an approach. Nixon then urged them to seek the Chinese Ambassador out at a social meeting. Stoessel did so at a Warsaw fashion show ballet performance.[1] Wang Li, a Chinese Foreign Service veteran, laughingly told us that Stoessel ran after the Chinese ambassador when he went to the men's room. There was no response, the State Department had reported back. Nixon concluded that the State Department was resistant to any change in policy. So he decided to shut the State Department out of the loop, and that included his old friend William Rogers out of any planning for any accommodation with China.

Indeed, the State Department could contend that the increasingly strident Anti-American rant that Mao was now spewing in 1969, in contrast to the more muted attacks on the United States by the Soviet Union, indicated the futility of any approach to China. Mao's air attack on U.S. planes in the Vietnam conflict in the summer of 1970 only fortified their arguments. Kissinger later stated "If the Chinese acted the way they talked during the Cultural Revolution, then it [the move toward China] was not doable."[2]

But if Nixon was to orchestrate this initiative from the White House, he had to do it with his National Security Council. In his meeting with President Johnson in December, 1968, the outgoing president had recommended that he should not revive that office. LBJ had discontinued it and relied totally on his Secretary of State Dean Rusk.

Nixon selected Henry Kissinger, the former Rockefeller advisor on foreign policy, to head the NSC even though Kissinger had let slip some disparaging remarks on Nixon's foreign policy capability. Despite that, Nixon had interviewed the Harvard educated Kissinger and was impressed by both his knowledge of Russia and its impact in history on Europe, as well as his familiarity, for an academic, with modern weapons technology.

A member of Kissinger's National Security Council once told James Humes after a tongue lashing by Kissinger: "Henry is an exaggerated Nixon—more brilliant, more paranoid, and more insecure." If Nixon thought he was looked down on by the prep-schooled Ivy League Eastern Establishment types, think of how a German born Jew with a heavy accent like Kissinger felt.

Yet there were significant differences. Kissinger had a witty charm that enabled him to 'schmooze'—offering anecdotal tidbits that would brighten a writer's column. Nixon, who had come to distrust the press—particularly after the 1960 campaign, was stiff and guarded. He was really an introvert in an extrovert's profession. (One incident that embittered him was in September, 1960, when he went to Duke University to give a speech on civil rights, in contrast to Senator Kennedy who never mentioned civil rights in the South, and the *New York Times* featured it as "Nixon Goes South to Garner Anti-Catholic Votes.")

Kissinger also typified the Teutonic trait of fawning before superiors like subjects before monarchs, and kicking subordinates like mongrel dogs. Professor Humes remembers Kissinger showing a toast he (Humes) had written for a head of government, "Did you write this piece of excrement?" as he ripped it up in front of him and his in-laws who were visiting. On another occasion, when Humes was with Kissinger's Deputy, Alexander Haig (then a colonel), Kissinger entered and Haig stood up and saluted. Nixon, on the other hand, was unfailingly considerate of staff and their families. (Haig would be awarded his general's star in 1971, just before he went to Beijing to follow up the Kissinger visit.)

Kissinger spent his formative years in Germany. He was a European whose sea was the Atlantic and whose sport was soccer.

Nixon grew up almost half a globe to the west, playing high school and college football, and wading in the surf of the Pacific, where he would serve as a Lieutenant Commander in World War II. China, the turmoil-riven giant of a nation on the other side fascinated him. Kissinger's interest and knowledge of China was only marginally less than that of the moon.

When Kissinger told Chou En-lai that the State Department was pro-Soviet he could have been describing himself. His interests were Soviet relations and the politics of missile weaponry. He saw his dominant priority, as Nixon's National Security head, to work out a détente with the Soviet Union and secure a mutual accord in strategic arms limitation. A move towards China, he believed, would threaten détente. The same month he took office, January, 1969, President Nixon told Dr. Kissinger that of the many projects facing them he wanted China to be given very high priority. Kissinger went down to the office of his Deputy Secretary of National Security, Colonel Alexander Haig, who remembers: "I recall Henry coming down from the Oval Office—'Al, this fellow wants to open relations with China. I think he has lost control of his senses.'"[3]

The Soviets, hungry for U.S. high tech machinery, were eager to meet the newly elected Nixon in a summit conference. The last one had been with LBJ in Glassboro, N.J., in 1967. The Russians believed that America's bargaining position had been weakened by the conflict in Vietnam.

Nixon brushed off any feelers for a summit. To any conference with the Soviets he wanted to go to the negotiating table with a strong hand.

To while away his idle days in the South Pacific, Nixon played poker. (His winnings helped him finance his younger brother's education at Duke University.) Later, in poker terms, he said he wanted to have two kings showing on the table as he bet.

The two face cards would be the military one of ABM (Anti-Ballistic Missile) defense system and the diplomatic one of an opening to China. He won passage of the ABM vote in the Democratic Senate in 1970, only by Vice President Agnew breaking a tie vote.

The China card would be far more difficult to achieve.

Professor Humes later asked the former president in his New Jersey office in 1980, "Mr. President, was winning the pact with Red China like wooing a nun?" Nixon nodded and started to laugh but his political reflexes triggered a belated frown. He had too many good Catholic friends. Then with a smile he quoted a Confucian bit of wisdom he had picked up from Chou En-lai "Desire to have things done quickly prevents their being done thoroughly."

Nixon had to cloak his overtures under a blanket of secrecy. The prying eyes of the State Department was rigid in its analysis of the People's Republic, insisting that only if the United States ended the Vietnam War and conceded Taiwan to the People's Republic could access to China be established.

Nixon's instinct told him otherwise. Despite the fact that the People's Republic was a sister Communist nation, Nixon knew through his studies and travels that historically the Chinese distrusted Russia. Nixon also suspected that Chinese attitudes were equally ambivalent towards the Vietnamese. China would not celebrate if a victorious North Vietnam would extend their military hegemony to Laos and Cambodia. Only Taiwan would be a problem with the Red Chinese.

Over Kissinger's objections, Nixon sent a signal to China in February, 1970, in the detailed Foreign Policy Report to Congress. It was this statement: "It is certainly in our interest, and in the interest of peace and stability in Asia and the world, that we take what steps we can toward improved practical relations with Beijing."[4]

In April, 1970, Nixon, by executive order, freed for export to China goods manufactured in other countries with American components and in July he lifted restrictions that for twenty years had prohibited American oil companies from refueling ships bound for China. These steps were not unnoticed by Chou En-lai.

In a trip to Romania, the previous August, Nixon had communicated his desire for a U.S. shift in Chinese policy. The Romanian dictator Nicolae Ceausceu, who had distanced himself from the Soviet Union, had been warmly received by Mao in China in 1968. Nixon was not only paying back Ceausceu's hospitality to the out-of-office Nixon in 1967, but more importantly he was asking the Romanian leader to use his 'good offices' to urge on Mao some accessibility to the new U.S. president

In October, 1970, the Chinese responded by the subtlest of signals. The American writer, Edgar Snow—an old friend of the Chinese Communists—stood beside Chairman Mao in the October 1 holiday parade. Before Nixon appreciated the significance of Snow's appearance with Mao—a muted gesture so typical of the deft hand of Chou—the president in an October interview with *TIME* magazine sent another signal saying: "If there is anything I want to do before I die, it is to go to China. If I don't, I want my children to."[5]

The Nixon Foreign Policy Statement officially confirmed what his stated hope to visit China and his talks with Ceausceu had implied. The signals were registering with Chou En-lai in Beijing.

The next step in Nixon's carefully orchestrated escalation of signals was to toast President Ceausceu on his return state visit in October, 1970, to the United States. Nixon referred to the leader as "a friend of the People's Republic of China." It was the first time a U.S. president had publicly spoken the words "People's Republic of China."[6] The American press did not pick it up but it was duly noted in Beijing.

Besides Romania, the leaders of two other countries were sounded out for advice and assistance. President deGaulle in France was one. After all, it was he who first suggested that if Nixon returned to the White House he should consider an opening to China.

President Yahya Khan of Pakistan was the other. Pakistan's principal adversary on the globe was neighboring India. India, which bordered China, had thorny relations with its huge Asian neighbor. The result was that Pakistan nursed close relations with China.

These three presidents directed their envoys in Beijing to point out to Chou En-lai these signals by Nixon.

For the first time back channels would not be used. In December, 1970, Nixon sent a message directly to China indicating his willingness to send an envoy. Time stood still, months passed. Nixon fretted that his initiative might have failed.

In 1971, Mao in privately pointing to the Soviet Union as their "major threat," concluded that it was time to open relations with the capitalist giant of America. It was Chou En-lai who would make it happen.

Mao was the power but Chou En-lai was the manipulator of that power.

A Nixon pantheon of life-size statues greets visitors to the Nixon Presidential Library in Yorba Linda, California. It is Chou En-lai, not Mao, who stands with Winston Churchill, Charles deGaulle, Konrad Adenauer, and Golda Meir.

In the book *Leaders*, which Nixon inscribed to Professor Humes in New York in 1980, the former president describes Chou En-lai: "Chou was a Communist revolutionary and a Confucian gentleman, a devoted ideologue and a calculating realist, a political infighter and a grand conciliator."[7]

Nixon responded to the Chinese moves by lifting all restrictions on the use of passports for travel to China. If this exchange of volleys across the Pacific by the U.S. and China suggest a game of Ping-Pong, it was fitting that the Chinese Reds first surfaced publicly with an invitation to the U.S. Ping-Pong team, which had been competing in Nagoya, Japan in April, 1971, to come to Beijing the next week.[8] Chou received the delegation of American table tennis players in the Great Hall of the People. Few western diplomats stationed in Beijing had ever been accorded this high honor.

Chou En-lai greeted them saying "You have opened a new page in the relations of the Chinese and American peoples. I am confident that this beginning again of our friendship will certainly meet with majority support of our two peoples."

When the stunned athletes did not respond, the Premier pressed the subject: "Don't you agree with me?" The Americans burst into applause and its captain promptly asked the Chinese team to tour the United States.

Chou En-lai chose the athletes because they had no political coloration and thus would trigger no negative spins in either of the two countries, and would also show the new friendly face of China to the world. By this ceremonial reception, Chou En-lai, on behalf of the People's Republic, had issued a public answer to a calibrated series of hints, gestures, and signals by Nixon. Vice-President Spiro Agnew, who knew nothing of the China plans, publicly criticized the activities as a "propaganda triumph for the Chinese"—and was promptly told to keep quiet.[9]

Chou En-lai communicated a response through President Yahya Khan of Pakistan. Chou stressed that the message did not come from him alone, but was the wish of Chairman Mao. With characteristic subtlety Chou concluded with a play on words, "We have had messages to and from the United States in the past", he said, "but this is the first time the proposal has come from a Head [of government] through a Head [of government] to a Head [of government]."[10] In other words, from Mao to Khan to Nixon.

On June 2, 1971, the Pakistan ambassador in Washington relayed Chou En-lai's invitation. Dr. Kissinger delivered the top secret message to President Nixon who was in the Lincoln sitting room, saying with his voice trembling, "Mr. President, this is the most important message that a president has received since World War II."[11] He called it a "diplomatic revolution."

Twenty-six days later, on June 28, 1971, Kissinger had expanded his estimate of the importance of the situation. According to Nixon's Chief of Staff, H.R. Haldeman, in his diary entry for that day: "The President made the comment that we're sitting now at a great watershed in history, clearly the greatest since World War II. Henry interjected that he considered it to be the greatest since the Civil War, as far as the overall effect on the nation."[12]

The popular belief is that in the building of the bridge to China, Nixon was the architect and Kissinger the engineer. In Kissinger's memoirs he spins it to make future historians believe that he had performed both roles.

Actually, when the president informed Kissinger that he, Kissinger, would be the envoy to make the arrangements for the President's visit, Kissinger refused. He thought the secret dealings would destroy the chances of détente with the Soviet Union, which was his prime objective. He went to the home in Washington, D.C. of his German mentor, Fritz Kramer, and wept that his career would be destroyed. As Kramer's son told James Humes, his father reminded him of the Machiavellian maxim "With two enemies you help the lesser one." Kissinger was not convinced and he went back to Nixon to reveal his misgivings. Nixon countered by saying he would send Secretary of State William Rogers. Kissinger immediately relented and agreed to go.

The conventional wisdom is that only a 'hard right wing Republican' could have initiated the opening to Red China. Indeed, *"Only Nixon"* is the title of this work. Yet to call Nixon 'right wing' is misleading. In fact, his domestic record of accomplishments is the most progressive record of any president since LBJ. Consider that Nixon initiated the amendment to give the District of Columbia a vote in presidential elections, and the legislation to end the military draft. In addition, it was Nixon who first initiated, by executive order, affirmative action in Federal contracts. Nixon also set up the Environmental Protection Agency. In addition he proposed the radical reform of Federal Family Assistance which would have established guaranteed income instead of the dole, but congressional Democrats opposed it. Finally, almost ninety per cent of school integration in the South was instituted by plans approved by the Nixon Justice Department.

Yet if 'only Nixon' means one who combined strong anti-communist credentials with an unparalleled experience in studies, travels, and meetings with world leaders, the phrase is accurate.

Nixon also possessed political courage. His decision to open relations with China was that of a statesman, not the usual status quo of a stand-pat politician. It was a huge risk. As Kissinger indicated in his memoirs, "Having made the decisions without executive or congressional consultation, Nixon had left himself quite naked should anything go wrong. In such lonely decisions he was extremely courageous."[13] As Nixon had played college football and basketball at Whittier College, and enjoyed watching baseball as his favorite relaxation, he was almost certainly aware of the basketball axiom "You miss 100% of the shots you never take."

Kissinger may have earlier believed that any overture to China would have destroyed his career, but by the time of the trip he was beginning to relish his role as a participant in this history making event. Kissinger left on July 1, 1971, with an itinerary that stopped at Saigon, Bangkok, and New Delhi, before arriving at Islamabad in Pakistan. The secret flight from there to Beijing was the stuff of any Hollywood or novel cloak and dagger thriller.

In Pakistan with the full cooperation of President Khan, Kissinger feigned a stomach illness after a state dinner. In the July 9-11 period while he was supposed to be in bed, he was flown to Beijing. He boarded at night wearing dark glasses and a hat.[14]

Just before Kissinger arrived in Pakistan, Nixon, in a presidential briefing on foreign policy in Kansas City, departed from the prepared text of remarks and told the assembled reporters:

> The goal of U.S. policy must be in the long term ending the isolation of Mainland China and a normalization of our relations with Mainland China. . . . Mainland China outside the world community completely isolated with its leaders not in communication with world leaders, would be a danger to the whole world that would be unacceptable. So, consequently this step must be taken now.[15]

Astonishingly all of the Washington press corps failed to follow up on the statement.[16] The same mistake was not made in Beijing, which received a full transcript by a back channel. When Kissinger arrived, he was embarrassed that he could not answer questions by Chou En-lai about the Kansas City remarks which he had not read.[17]

Kissinger's negotiations with Premier Chou En-lai were successful. Before leaving Chou told Kissinger "Once the announcement is made it will shake the world, which won't be able to sleep."[18]

President Nixon had once said that unpredictability is the greatest asset or weapon that a leader can have.[19] This was to be demonstrated shortly after Kissinger returned from the secret trip to Beijing.

On July 15, 1971, President Nixon delivered on television a three minute announcement that he had accepted an invitation from the Chinese Premier to visit Beijing "to seek the normalization of relations between the two countries and to exchange questions of concern between the two sides."[20]

An America, weary with the Vietnam conflict, was dumbstruck. Leftist communist Max Lerner wrote "The Politics of Surprise lead through the Gates of Astonishment into the Kingdom of Hope."[21]

In London, former British Prime Minister Harold Macmillan cited the historic comment of the nineteenth century British statesman George Canning [in helping the Americans to declare the Monroe Doctrine]: "I have brought the new world into existence to redress the balance of the old" and added that Nixon had reversed Canning—"he's brought the oldest civilization in the world back into the game to redress the new Russian empire."[22]

In Moscow, as expected, the news shocked the Central Committee of the Communist Party. Georgi Arbatov, the advisor on U.S. Affairs for the U.S.S.R., heard stunned colleagues say things like:

America will be China's ally.

Kissinger—what else has he agreed?

When Nixon visits Beijing anything could happen.

All this will make things very difficult for us.
Where will it all end?[23]

Nixon's gamble worked. Four days after his announcement the Kremlin invited the President to Moscow—the long stalled arms talks would now proceed.[24]

President Nixon explained in his own words: "As we moved closer to China, the Soviet Union didn't want to be left behind, they moved closer to us, so the Russian Game made the Chinese Game work, and the Chinese Game made the Russian Game work."[25]

In 1982, Professor Humes as a Woodrow Wilson Fellow at the Center for International Scholars at the Smithsonian, heard the aged Macmillan tell their group of scholars that the Nixon trip was "the diplomatic feat of the century."

Wikipedia ("the free encyclopedia of the internet") refers to the entry "Nixon in China": "The visit has become a metaphor for an *unexpected and uncharacteristic action by a politician.*"

Yet the world did not know that the visit was far from a sure thing. In September, 1971, an alleged coup attempt in China ended with the death of Mao's hand picked successor, Lin Biao, in a suspicious plane crash. Then many high ranking military leaders were replaced. To test the waters, a full scale dress rehearsal of the trip was mounted in January, 1972. Kissinger's Deputy in the National Security Council, General Alexander Haig, was sent, and as previously mentioned was snubbed and rebuffed. The 'Gang of Four' was trying to torpedo the Nixon visit. But Nixon had carefully laid the groundwork with Chou and Chou had Mao counter and block the moves of the 'Gang of Four'. Zhang Hanzhi, the interpreter for Mao and Chou En-lai who was with the group of Chinese accompanying the sabotaged boat trip in Hangzhou of General Haig, remembers well the reaction of Mao and Chou when they learned what the "Gang of Four" had done. She said that Chou "really criticized us very very seriously and said 'What happened in Shanghai and Hangzhou almost upset the whole strategy of Mao Tse-tung's plan of break *(sic)* the ice between the U.S. and China.'"[26]

Nixon left for James Humes, on his death, a small card entitled the Ten Commandments of Statecraft. Humes wrote a book of that title, discussing each of the Ten. The number one axiom read "Always Be Prepared to Negotiate but Never Negotiate without Being Prepared."[27]

Winston Churchill told A.B.A. president Charles Rhyne in 1957, when Churchill spoke at the Bar Association's meeting in London, that "Nixon was the best briefed and most prepared spokesman of the American government" he had ever met. Churchill said that Nixon was the only diplomatic visitor who ever received a standing ovation after a Q.&A. session with the press on that London visit in 1957. His grandson Winston Churchill II confirmed his grandfather's respect for Nixon's preparedness when he visited James Humes and Jarvis Ryals in Colorado in 2005.

James Humes was witness to the indefatigable research and study that took place before Vice-President Nixon made the visit to Moscow in 1959—i.e. Russia—biographies and novels read, Russian phrases for social amenities memorized, calls to everyone who had ever talked to Khrushchev, as well as 132 file cards about every issue that divided the U.S. and the U.S.S.R.

The preparation for the visit to China the following February was just as intense. Of those who knew Chairman Mao Tse-tung and Premier Chou En-lai, Nixon was profoundly impressed with the advice of Andre Malraux, whom President deGaulle had urged the American president to talk to before he left for China. Malraux was a French novelist and confidant of deGaulle.

As Jonathan Aitken, the Nixon biographer, related to Professor Humes in London, "Nixon was taken with Malraux. Among other things he presented this portrait of Mao Tse-tung:

> You will meet a man who believes he has a fantastic destiny and who believes that he is acting out the last act of his lifetime. You may think he is talking to you but in truth he will be addressing Death. You will be dealing with a colossus, but a colossus facing death."[28]

In his own memoirs Nixon was struck with Malraux's poignant words to him as the French author was at the door to leave the Oval Office:

> You are about to attempt one of the most important things of our century. I think of the sixteenth century explorers, who set out for a specific objective but often arrived at an entirely different discovery. I am not deGaulle but I know what deGaulle would say if he were here. He would say "All men who understand what you are embarking upon, salute you!"[29]

When the former president repeated Malraux's words to Professor Humes in his New York apartment on the East Side in 1980, the author could note some tears in his eyes and hoarseness in his voice. Nixon also relayed some of the French writer's comments on Chou En-lai—which would be confirmed when Nixon met him later:

> If Mao is the peasant-philosopher, Chou En-lai is the cosmopolitan diplomat. His years as an envoy in Paris has left him with an appreciation of the finer things of life. But don't mistake his suavity for softness. Velvet covers steel.

One serious concern was the fact that President Nixon was taking off without any promise of an appointment with Chairman Mao. There were those, particularly from the State Department, who argued against a state visit by Nixon on that rationale—that the president might not meet chairman Mao. If Nixon failed to see the Chinese head of state it would be interpreted by the world as an egregious snub. The significance of the visit would have been dramatically diminished. Notwithstanding, Nixon decided to take the gamble. It took considerable nerve for him to press on at a time when the Cultural Revolution was still in progress and the stability of the country in question.[30]

The former Deputy Foreign Secretary, Guo Jiading, told the three of us why no assurance of a meeting by President Nixon with Chairman Mao was tendered. The reason was not for matters of foreign policy but for the feebleness of the Chairman's health. Throughout the fall of 1971 Mao was bed ridden, surrounded by nurses, oxygen tanks, and ventilation equipment.[31]

Yet when the president's plane touched down in Beijing on February 21, 1972, Mao summoned the strength to struggle out of bed, ordering the removal of the nurses and the medical gear he issued the command "Bring Nixon here now."[32]

Nixon in *Leaders* described him on that first meeting "robust, earthy, exuding an animal magnetism."[33] Nixon recalled in 1977 that Mao said "I see where your friend Chiang Kai-shek called me a bandit."

After the translation Nixon said "What does the Chairman call Chiang Kai-shek?"

Nixon stated Mao said "Well, uh, I call him a bandit too." Then Chou En-lai said "We just abuse each other." Then both Mao and Chou threw their heads back and laughed.[34]

Nixon then said "You are aware of my sentiments in regard to communism. I am considered to be a rightist."

Then Mao said "I like rightists. I like Prime Minister Heath. I voted for you."

Nixon then said "Sometimes those on the right can do things which those on the left can only talk about. I could do it because no one could question my so called anti-communist credentials."[35]

At the end of the meeting, Mao had to be helped to stand up for the handshake.[36]

Yet it was the proffered outstretched handshake President Nixon was extending as he descended the airplane steps to greet Premier Chou that would be forever etched in their collective memory. Secretary of State John Foster Dulles, in 1954 at the Geneva Conference, had refused to take Chou En-lai's hand and that snub still rankled the Chinese.[37] Nixon, who had done his diplomatic homework, understood that and was determined to begin the opening of relations with the People's Republic with this symbolic and dramatic shaking of hands.

On their ride from the airport into the city, Premier Chou said to President Nixon, "Your handshake came over the vastest ocean in the world—twenty-five years of no communication."[38]

NOTES

1. videotape
2. videotape
3. videotape
4. Nixon, *RN*, 545
5. Ibid., 546
6. Ibid.
7. Nixon, *Leaders*, 218
8. videotape
9. videotape
10. Nixon, *RN*, 547
11. Ibid., 552
12. Haldeman, 307
13. Kissinger, 734
14. videotape
15. Aitken, 428
16. Ibid.
17. Ibid., 429
18. videotape
19. Humes, 106
20. videotape
21. Nixon, *RN*, 554
22. Aitken, 429
23. videotape
24. videotape
25. videotape
26. videotape
27. Humes, 29
28. Nixon, *RN*, 558
29. Ibid., 558, 559
30. Aitken, 430, 431
31. Ibid., 431
32. Ibid.
33. Nixon, *Leaders*, 238

34. videotape
35. videotape
36. videotape
37. Nixon, *Leaders*, 224
38. Nixon, *RN*, 560

Chapter Seven

"Only a Republican President"

"America was a hero with clay feet." These were the words of a former Mayor of Shanghai to the authors at a luncheon for our party on October 1, 1998. This acid observation described the disillusionment of Chinese with the United States in developments following the defeat of Japan in 1945. Alone of the western nations, the United States had housed no mercantile center in the Bund in Shanghai such as Britain, Germany, or France. Neither did America administer exploitive colonies in Asia as the British, French, and Dutch.

The speaker, Li-Kwan-Chou, who was in his ninetieth year, was still erect in posture and lucid in mind even if his voice was halting in delivery. He had been approaching thirty when the Japanese armies invaded his native city. Then when the United States declared war against Japan at the time of Pearl Harbor, he, like other Chinese, had faith that the Americans would be their liberators. But then after the war, he said, the United States chose to side with "the corrupt Chiang Kai-shek."

A week earlier in our trip, Ambassador Zhang Yijun at the Government Office in Beijing had mentioned the irony of the United States' advocacy of Chiang Kai-shek. Chiang Kai-shek, he said, had been "Moscow's man." From the 1930's to just after the war ended, Stalin had backed Chiang over Mao Tse-tung.

In 1945, Mao, related Ambassador Zhang, still put his trust in America. He had established a good working relationship with General Joseph Stilwell. Stilwell, nicknamed "Vinegar Joe," was vitriolic in his appraisement of the inflated posturing of the self-styled Generalissimo Chiang Kai-shek.[1] But Chiang had ingratiated himself with U.S. Ambassador to China, Pat Hurley, a former Secretary of War under President Herbert Hoover. In America it was the Generalissimo and his American educated Madame Chiang who had captured the American fancy. The Chinese power duo had made friends with Nobel Prize winner novelist of China, Pearl Buck. In American eyes Chiang had become the face of China, just as Stalin embodied Russia, and Churchill personified Britain.

Zhang speculated to us that if America had befriended Mao, he might well have become "a super Tito," that is, a fellow antagonist of the U.S.S.R., if not actually an ally of the United States.

Historian Barbara Tuchman in her news-making essay, "If Mao Had Come to Washington in 1945: An Essay in Alternatives" in *Foreign Affairs*, October, 1972, relates how Mao and Chou En-lai both wanted to come to Washington D.C. in 1945 to meet with President Franklin D. Roosevelt, but the message never was passed on by Ambassador Hurley in the embassy in China. Twenty-seven years later, after two wars and millions of lives lost, an American President reversed the unmade journey of 1945 and traveled to Beijing to meet those same two Chinese leaders.[2]

Tuchman speculated about how such a meeting—which did not take place—might have changed the course of postwar history including a possible avoidance of three years of civil war and the resulting Taiwan situation, as well as obviating the years of harm caused by mutual suspicion and fears between two great powers not on speaking terms. Posssibly, suggested Tuchman, there might have been no Korean or Vietnam wars. As early as May, 1941, an unpublished policy study of the Council on Foreign Relations made explicit the goal of the United States by stating: "It is vital that there be no civil war in China."[3]

Like all those we interviewed, Zhang was a dedicated Communist. The Party had been his career and his life. But by 1998 the tenets of Marxism had been distorted almost beyond recognition in the government's new programs for economic expansion. If their belief in the economic determinism of Communism had ebbed, their faith in the greatness of China and the future was unshaken.

It was once said that if the Germans believed they were the "master race," France thought they had the superior culture. In Asia the Japanese are the fanatical nationalists. The Chinese believe they invented civilization. The printing press, the novel, figure painting in art, and gunpowder (a dubious contribution to some) all were first introduced by the Chinese. Political scientists and bureaucrats respectively credit or curse the Chinese for requiring the first civil service examinations back in the seventh century.

Back in the time of Confucius, the Chinese called their empire "the Middle Kingdom" meaning the center of the world. In the present world, the Chinese still consider their one and a third billion population country as the central country on the globe.

But in the years following World War II, China felt they were "disrespected" by the country from which they most wanted respect. Almost everyone we interviewed mentioned the refusal of U.S. Secretary of State John Foster Dulles to shake the proffered hand of Premier Chou En-lai at the Geneva Conference in 1954. That rejection, etched in the minds and souls of Chinese, was an insult to their dignity and pride that could not be effaced.

One of those who mentioned the handshaking incident in Geneva was Ambassador Ji Chaozhu. He had been an English interpreter for both Mao Tse-tung and Chou En-lai. In 1998 he was close to seventy but looked fifteen years younger. He was relatively tall, for a Chinese, due to his better nutrition growing up in the United States. His longish face emphasized his height. But his spectacles, a wide grin, and frequent chuckles brightened his oblong facial features.

Ambassador Ji, who had been the interpreter for the Chinese Delegation to the Geneva Convention in 1954, was not laughing when he told us that Secretary of State John Foster Dulles had instructed Deputy Secretary of State General Walter Bedell Smith, as well as all departmental staff, not to shake hands with any of the Chinese attending the conference. At the first plenary session of the February, 1972, visit in the Great Hall of the People, Premier Chou mentioned that incident in 1954. He told the Americans "Dulles's assistant, Mr. Walter Bedell Smith, wanted to do differently, but he did not break the discipline of John Foster Dulles, so he had to hold a cup of coffee in his right hand. Since one doesn't shake hands with the left hand, he used it to shake my arm." Everyone laughed, including Chou. "But at that time, we couldn't blame you," he said, "because the international viewpoint was that the socialist countries were a monolithic bloc, and the Western countries were also a monolithic bloc. Now we understand that that is not the case."[4]

President Nixon responded, "We have broken out of the old pattern. We look at each country in terms of its own conduct rather than lumping them all together and saying that because they have this kind of philosophy they are all in utter darkness. I would say in honesty to the Prime Minister that my views, because I was in the Eisenhower administration, were similar to those of Mr. Dulles at that time. But the world has changed since then, and the relationship between the People's Republic and the United States must change too. As the Prime Minister has said in a meeting with Dr. Kissinger, the helmsman must ride with the waves or he will be submerged with the tide." By the time they all met an hour later for the banquet at the Great Hall of the People, the Chinese group seemed to be much more at ease.[5]

In his life from schoolboy to senior diplomat, Ambassador Ji personified the trajectory from disillusionment with the early American post-war treatment of Chinese to delight with the Nixon accommodation with the People's Republic almost three decades later.

After Japan invaded China in 1937, Ji's family suffered two years of hardship and danger before escaping in 1939. Ji was nine years old when the family was taken by his father, one of the most respected and revered scholars in China, to New York, arriving on February 3, 1939.[6] Ji was frequently called 'Little Ji,' as his father was the 'Elder Ji.' (Elder Ji was mentioned in Chapter Three as a victim of the Cultural Revolution.) In 1944 Little Ji entered Horace Mann-Lincoln, a progressive high school in New York City.[7] Little Ji believed that Mao and the Communists represented the future of China, and it was well known in school that he, himself, was a Communist. He drew unflattering caricatures of Chiang Kai-shek and President Truman on the blackboards, and his teachers merely dismissed them as most of them were leftists also.[8]

Interestingly, the 'Elder Ji' played the role of an old bearded Chinese doctor who saved the life of the American flyer Ted Lawson, played by Van Johnson, in the U.S. movie *Thirty Seconds over Tokyo*.[9] Spencer Tracy portrayed Jimmy Doolittle. In 1998, Little Ji told us his father was offered another part in the movie *The Purple Heart*, but because the film called for him to play the role of a Chinese traitor, he refused. Little Ji's chest "swelled with love and pride" when he saw his father in *Thirty Seconds over Tokyo* on the day the movie opened in November, 1944.[10] In January, 1946, Elder Ji returned to China to accept a position as dean of the law school at Peking University.[11]

Little Ji graduated from Horace Mann-Lincoln high school in 1948 and was admitted to Harvard University on a scholarship.[12] His ambition was to get his Ph.D. in chemistry and return to China to help rebuild his native land.[13] He and his fellow communist student friends were overjoyed by the founding of the People's Republic of China by Mao and Chou En-lai on October 1, 1949.[14] Several of these friends were summoned back to China to play important roles in the new government, and Ji felt "a powerful urge to return" but his "path was set."[15]

Little Ji realized his fortunate situation at Harvard and described himself as being "fully assimilated" with his "future secure."[16] He stayed in Cambridge the following summer, 1950, to take summer courses to give himself "a leg up."[17] When the Korean conflict broke out that summer he was dismayed—"the last thing the People's Republic needed in its first year of existence was a new war."[18]

The Soviet-backed North Korea invaded the U.S.-backed South, and because of an already signed mutual-assistance pact with the Soviets, China was pulled in.[19]

The U.S. at that time was alarmed that if the People's Republic seized Taiwan, U.S.- occupied Japan would be boxed in on three sides: the Communist Chinese mainland to the west, Communist North Korea to the north, and a Communist-controlled Taiwan to the south.[20] The People's Republic looked at the situation from the opposite side: if the U.S. "could maintain puppet regimes in South Korea and on Taiwan, China would have a wolf sleeping on its stoop."[21]

Little Ji, and most Chinese, held the belief that "China is too often portrayed in the Western press as a threat when, in fact, the Chinese worldview is traditionally inward-looking and defensive rather than imperialistic."[22] He and his friends were outraged that the U.S. reversed an announced policy and gave support to the "bandit" Chiang Kai-shek, who was despised as a corrupt foe of the People's Republic. Taiwan had been a part of China until in the 1890's when Japan seized it and forced the Qing dynasty to surrender control, so China had bonafide historical claims to consider the island as part of their country.[23]

Little Ji was horrified that the two countries he loved, and considered "his own," were moving rapidly toward conflict with each other. He described a "deeply personal crisis" that preoccupied his "every waking moment" about what he should do—the powerful urge to return to his first homeland and probable real danger or to remain with his future secured as a Harvard scholarship student and life in the U.S.[24]

Ji's agony was exacerbated by the growing anti-red hysteria stirred up by Senator Joseph McCarthy.[25]

After wrestling with his dilemma for weeks trying to determine what to do, the decision came to him suddenly as an epiphany one "moonlit evening in early September, 1950," at age 21. Ji and some friends were walking back to their dorms from classes when they heard the notes of Beethoven's Piano Concerto Number Five, the "Emperor," coming through an open window. The music seemed to be slowly dying to a conclusion, but from a whisper it began to swell and was joined by a chorus of strings, and then the entire orchestra built up to a mighty crescendo in the finale.

Ji wrote that the music seemed to vibrate in his bones: His "chest tightened, his brain tingled, and he felt a flush over his neck and scalp." He then shouted only two words to his surprised friends—"Gotta run"—then sprinted back to his room, packed an overnight bag and caught the night train to New York where he told his mother of his decision to return to China.[26]

Ambassador Ji Chaozhu's new book, *The Man on Mao's Right: From Harvard Yard to Tiananmen Square, My Life inside China's Foreign Ministry*, was published in July, 2008, at the time of the completion of the manuscript for *"Only Nixon."* In it he documents his years of struggle and hardship as a student, his stint as a translator at the Panmunjom Korean armistice talks, as an interpreter at the 1954 Geneva peace talks, then his see-saw climb through the People's Republic's foreign office bureaucracy— with times sent to the country for hard manual labor to renew his 'revolutionary spirit.' He would eventually rise to become a translator for both Chou En-lai and Mao. Ji well describes the horrors of the Great Leap Forward and the Great Proletarian Cultural Revolution. His career culminated with the position of Ambassador to the Court of St. James—the United Kingdom—for four years, then for five years as under secretary-general of the United Nations for Economic and Social Development.[27]

'Little Ji' beamed with pride as he recalled his standing behind Premier Chou En-lai at the time President Nixon extended his outreached hand. We then showed him a small paperback book with pictures entitled *The President's Trip to China* which did, indeed, portray him right in back of Premier Chou during "The Handshake that Shook the World." He was visibly moved at the photographic evidence of his presence at this climactic moment in history and wiped his face with his handkerchief. He asked if it would be possible to get him a copy of the picture, and we assured him we would do everything possible to get one for him. After our return to the U.S., Edward Nixon contacted the publisher of the paperback and obtained a copy of it and we mailed it to him. (This picture is # 14 in *"Only Nixon."*)

In his book Ambassador Ji relates that the day after the above picture was made, in photos released to the Chinese press, he (Ji) was airbrushed out of the picture and the picture of Chairman Mao's grandniece was substituted.[28] Another example of the erratic and treacherous nature of Chinese political maneuvers at that time occurred this same year Little Ji was the interpreter for the historic meeting of Premier Chou En-lai and President Nixon in 1972. Only a few months later he was ordered back to labor in the fields for another round of "peasant reeducation." His physical health made his field work punishment of transplanting rice seedlings so feeble and slow that the "authorities at the cadre school" switched his assignment to "weeding out hidden counterrevolutionaries" and the "politically impure". Fortunately, he was rescued after a short time when Premier Chou asked "Where has Little Ji gone? I need him!" so he was summoned back to Beijing in the late summer of 1972.[29]

The first signal to Little Ji that Nixon would be a different president, was when he read in his Inaugural Address—which he showed to Chou En-lai— that the U.S. president said he would be "open to all nations." Although the New China Agency, the government's press arm, ridiculed the words, Ji thought it bore real significance.

Chou En-lai said to Little Ji at the time that he didn't think Nixon was the war-monger the left had portrayed, but was a 'peace maker.' Then, said Little

Ji, the Chinese premier had quoted a cryptic line from Confucius to describe his instinctive impression of Nixon: "Men of principle are sure to be bold, but those who are bold are not always men of principle."

Wang Li was a distinguished man with white hair and quiet presence that projected authority. He had recently published a book, *The Diplomatic History of Sino-U.S. Relations,* and had noted even earlier a cue from Richard Nixon that his presidency could pre-sage a new and different chapter in America's relations with the People's Republic. Wang Li, who would end his diplomatic career as Consul-General in Chicago, had been taken by a press conference of the newly nominated Nixon at the Republican Convention in Miami on August 9, 1968.

In it Nixon stated "We cannot forget China. We must seek to negotiate with China. We should not wait silently but push for change." Wang Li read that from his book. But then he quoted by memory Nixon's words in his Inaugural: "Let every country know that during this Administration we will seek ways to communicate openly to all countries." And then Wang Li added the Nixon words that soon followed: "We seek an open world where no people great or small live in angry isolation." This, said Wang Li, was addressed directly to the Chinese.

Soon after that, Mao and Chou En-lai called a meeting of the four top Red Army marshals and generals, who all had been with Mao on the Long March, and asked them their thoughts on reassessing their relations with the United States. They recommended that China should move back towards the U.S. Afterwards, Chou En-lai told Wang Li and other English-speaking specialists to watch out "for any more feelers" from Nixon.

For our principal host throughout the trip, the jovial Zhang Yijun, the big signal was President Nixon's Kansas City speech in 1971. Zhang Yijun had been the advance man for the Nixon trip in 1972 and would end his career as Ambassador to Canada. But in 1971, Zhang Yijun was working in the Ministry of Foreign Affairs. Chou En-lai told him to study Nixon's speech and write a memorandum on it. In this address to the World Affairs Council of Kansas City, Nixon outlined "Five Powers of Influence"—U.S., U.S.S.R., Europe, Japan, and China. What Zhang Yijun did not know at that time was that Henry Kissinger was already en route on the secret trip from Pakistan to the People's Republic. Zhang related that Chou En-lai would be bemused by the fact that Kissinger did not know of the Kansas City speech. It confirmed Chou En-lai's belief that Nixon himself was the real architect of the new China policy, and that Kissinger was the messenger as well as the diplomat who would have to work out the details.

For Mme. Zi Zhongyun the announcement of the Nixon visit came as a bolt out of the blue—literally. Because of the Cultural Revolution she was compelled to do farm work, and was at the time plowing a field under the skies of Hunan. She was not in the Foreign Office in Beijing, where she would have been in the position to have digested certain cues or feelers. A fellow candidate for "re-education" in her camp had informed her of the scheduled Nixon trip and they came in from the field to listen to the radio, which had reported the upcoming Kissinger visit to Beijing.

Mme. Zi Zhongyun, although a slightly built, short Asian female, was a no-nonsense woman with a comfortable presence who looked like she could write reports or bake cookies with equal skill. Still, it was hard to imagine this ninety pound woman ever personally pulling a plow in the fields. But she had. When she talked of plowing the fields, one of our group commented that walking behind a horse pulling a plow was hard work. She was surprised at our lack of understanding and said: "What horses? *We* pulled the plows!" Now in her seventies she was writing a book on the twentieth century U.S. presidency from Theodore Roosevelt to Ronald Reagan.

Mme. Zi recalled that in the fall of 1971 when she was working in the wheat fields, she had just about given up all hope. She was convinced she would die in that "re-education camp," where the days were spent plowing the fields and the evenings "listening to military representatives of the People's Liberation Army lecturing them on Engels, Marx, and Mao."

Shortly after she heard the news of the scheduled Kissinger trip, there was an official order transmitted to them of the interview between Chairman Mao and Edgar Snow, the pro-People's Republic American writer, in which it was stated that "President Nixon could come anytime" he wished. She was stunned. But to the Chinese, Mao was God. If Mao said it was right for Nixon to come, then it was right.

Mao may have said that he did not want to be a 'cult figure,' but he was, despite his protestations. To the Chinese people, Mao was that huge poster picture adorning the exhibition building in Tiananmen Square—like a George Washington on the dollar bill. Mao, the father of the People's Republic, was as remote a figure as the father of our country. In the early days of our republic, Jefferson, Madison, and Hamilton were approachable, just as Chou En-lai was to the Foreign Service professionals, but Washington was a god-like figure. Similarly, like the General in the winter at Valley Forge, the General who weathered the Long March was a myth-like man of epic proportions.

Ambassador Ji describes Mao as "remote and inaccessible," and even "crude."[30] In contrast he views Premier Chou as "warm and human." Little Ji echoed the assessment of Malraux (in Chapter Six) of Premier Chou being a "cosmopolitan diplomat," by describing him as "principled but flexible, dignified but gracious, a gentleman but also a realist."[31]

The Articles of Confederation was the U.S. national charter until General Washington's appearance at the Constitutional Convention negated it. In the same way, Mao's decision to welcome Nixon wiped out, in one stroke, the party pronouncements against the "imperialist and capitalist dog America."

It was Chou En-lai who summoned Mme. Zi Zhongyun back to Beijing. He wanted the insight of those who understood English and western ways. At that time Mme. Zi's fluent French was much better than her barely passable English, but in Beijing she hastened to catch up. She was convinced Chou En-lai had overlooked the English requirement to rescue her from her dead-end situation.

Mme. Zi Zhongyun stressed to us, that without Chou, the Nixon visit would never have taken place. "The Gang of Four" was ruthless in their opposition and would have considered assassination and murder if necessary. She let that slip when she discussed the famous Ping-Pong tournament where the U.S. would be playing along with the Chinese. Chou En-lai had ordered that the group be split into two groups and two planes, because of fears that the "Gang of Four" might sabotage or shoot down the one plane.

In our very first interview on September 22, former Ambassador Guo Jiading, now the Executive Vice-President of the Pacific Economic Cooperation Commission gave us the first indication of the respect Premier Chou En-lai was held in by the Chinese Foreign Service elite. Guo Jiading, a diminutive man with a triangular face, looked his age of seventy-five despite his black hair. Chou En-lai, Guo Jiading pointed out, was among the first to sense that Nixon was a president they could deal with. Chou said "the Democrats—such as presidents Kennedy and Johnson—were too sensitive to accusations of 'appeasement,' and would bend over backwards to prove differently."

Little Ji would repeat Chou's assessment of Nixon stating that "it would be easier for a Republican president to bring about a rapprochement with China than a Democrat."

Ji, a raconteur of no mean ability, also recounted an anecdote about Chou that underscored the Premier's prowess in language skills. Chou En-lai, in a world conference, made a toast to peace in Chinese. The English interpreter then said it in English, whereupon Chou En-lai corrected one word. Then the Chinese-French interpreter delivered the toast in French, and again Chou substituted a better French word for the one used. The Japanese interpreter then delivered the toast in that language, and again Chou corrected one word. The Russian interpreter now gave a translation, and yet again Chou amended it with a one word correction. But when the Chinese Arabic expert delivered the toast in Arabic, everyone looked to Chou, who sat quietly and then slowly a sly smile began to creep onto his face—then he joined everyone else in laughter. Arabic was one language Chou could not speak.

Ambassador Tang Longbin was another of the interviewees who had a particular esteem for Chou En-lai. Tang Longbin was dwarfed by at least a foot next to Ed Nixon's 6'4". His title came from the English-speaking countries he had served as envoy—Britain, Australia, and Canada. He spoke English in a carefully modulated British accent which added authority to his unimposing appearance. Some of the anecdotes he related about Chou were a testament to the tact and consideration he revealed as a host.

For one thing, in a dinner in which President Nixon would have to make repeated toasts to Mao, the Chinese people, and their contributions to civilization, Chou put a lit match to the fiery Mai Tai made from sorghum and water with about 67% alcohol content. This was a signal to Nixon of its highly intoxicating effect and to sip it very slowly.

On another occasion Chou issued the order to the souvenir shops (put together for the purpose of the President's visit) to bring their wares to the hotels where Nixon's around-the-clock working White House staffers were staying. This was so they could take some gifts back to their wives and families, since they would not have the time to go souvenir shopping.

Chou En-lai had made himself familiar with American customs and habits. To cite one example, he related how when a waitress served Chou En-lai first at the initial banquet, he directed them to first attend Mrs. Nixon, and then the President, which was the U.S. protocol.

Chou, Ambassador Tang said, took special efforts to exert his charm and humor on Mrs. Nixon. During the State Banquet the cigarette-smoking Chou offered a cigarette to Mrs. Nixon, who also smoked. "Will you have a Panda?" he asked. 'Panda' is the name of the state-manufactured cigarettes in China. When she said "Yes, thank you," Chou used that play on words to break the news that they would be sending two panda bears to America as their gift to her and the president. He knew that panda bears were only second to teddy bears as the choice for children's bedtime companions.

Chou En-lai's knowledge of America even extended to its popular and familiar songs. Nixon, he knew, liked to play the piano. And what he used to play were not sonatas by Beethoven, but old songs to entertain his dinner guests. Accordingly, Chou chose for the band to play "Home on the Range", "Turkey in the Straw", "Don't Sit under the Apple Tree", and Tang thought "The Sunny Side of the Street." Nixon was so pleased with the selections that he walked about fifty yards across the vast Dining Room that was seating 5,000 people to thank the musicians.

Ambassador Tang took great pride that he was selected to accompany Henry Kissinger on the 4 ½ hour secret trip from Islamabad, Pakistan, that arrived at 8:00 AM in Beijing.[32] Tang had made a trial flight the month before to check out the flight time.

He was also with Chou En-lai at 5PM, February 27, 1972, in Shanghai when Kissinger announced the Shanghai Communiqué. It was Premier Chou, said Tang, who graciously let Kissinger announce it five minutes before the Chinese did so.

Like some of the others we interviewed, Tang saw that Henry Kissinger could turn on the charm and sense of humor just like Chou. He remembered how Kissinger would tease Nancy Tang, Mao's interpreter: "It's not fair that you could be elected president of the United States, and I can't."[33] Nancy Tang, the daughter of a Chinese diplomat, had been born in America and lived the first eight and a half years of her life in Brooklyn. Accordingly, she spoke with an American accent.[34] Interestingly, in 1985 when James Humes was in the People's Republic doing a series of lectures to Chinese universities, he was the guest at a reception given by the Cultural Affairs Office at the U.S. Embassy officer's apartment. Suddenly a woman of about fifty came in and delivered a note to the guest. It was Nancy Tang. The American host was astonished. He had thought she was either dead or in prison somewhere, at the order of Chairman Deng Xiaoping. Tang asked Humes to deliver the message to President Nixon that she would ever revere him and respect his historic contribution. (Nancy Tang, incidentally, is supposedly the inspiration for the young Chinese woman, "Honey" Huan, in the *Doonesbury* cartoon strip.)

Nancy Tang made no mention of Dr. Kissinger. It was only Nixon she wanted to be remembered to. Henry Kissinger's spin of the historic trip was at variance with the Chinese we interviewed, who all knew that it was Nixon, born on the shores of the Pacific and not Kissinger raised in Germany, who conceived of the Beijing breakthrough.

More than one of those we talked to cited Kissinger's ignorance of President Nixon's Kansas City speech where he outlined "the new Five Spheres of Power" that included China.

Ambassador Qian Dayong, the Senior Research Fellow of the China Institute of International Studies, was a slight bookish scholar with glasses, who had made a career of Sino-American Relations. He pointed out to us on our second day in Beijing, that when Nixon wrote his provocative essay "Asia after Vietnam" in the spring of 1967, for publication that fall that outlined future initiatives in foreign policy, he had never met Henry Kissinger, who was then an expert on the Soviets working for Republican presidential candidate Nelson Rockefeller. This was the article Ambassador Qian Dayong said where Nixon stressed "any Asian policy must include China." By mid October, 1968, Nixon looked so assured of victory that he was even prepared to describe his future presidential plans for foreign affairs. In a conversation with Harrison Salisbury, the Assistant Managing Editor of the *New York Times* on October 18, 1968, Nixon mentioned he planned to make an opening to China. This conversation took place six weeks before Nixon met Henry Kissinger, thus conclusively answering the question as to who was the real architect of the Nixon-Kissinger China policy. It also demonstrated how much care and thought had gone into Nixon's preparations for the course he would later follow as president.[35]

Ambassador Guo Jiading, the day before, revealed a conversation Chou En-lai had with Dr. Kissinger in Beijing in October, 1971. Kissinger told him that in no way would China be admitted to the United Nations in 1971. Premier Chou smiled, knowing differently. Two days later China, over U.S. Ambassador to the U.N. George H.W. Bush's objection, was voted admission on October 11, 1971. The inference that Ambassador Guo made was that Kissinger was "clearly out of the loop." Chou En-lai had said to him that it was his belief that Nixon passed the word to some of our allies in the U.N.— if not to Kissinger and Bush—that he was taking a hands-off-policy, even though the U.S. would vote 'no.'

Ambassador Wang Li, the distinguished author of *The Diplomatic History of Sino-U.S. Relations*, let slip one of the most significant findings by Chinese Intelligence. They had the transcript of a telephone call made by U.S. Ambassador Arthur Hartman in Moscow to Kissinger in his National Security Office in the White House in November, 1970. In it Hartman strongly argued against any opening of U.S. relations with China, on the basis that it would jeopardize any possibility of détente, as well as progress on the S.A.L.T. talks with the Soviet Union in limiting nuclear missiles. Kissinger replied "I couldn't agree with you more." In Wang Li's words, it proved that "Kissinger was a limited Europeanist," unlike Nixon.

Kissinger, in his spin of the historic trip in his memoir *White House Years*, gives somewhat grudging credit to Nixon while showing a different posture from the response to Ambassador Hartman noted above, and the words to Col. Haig at the beginning of the Nixon presidency noted earlier. He states about Nixon: "He had thought up the China initiative (even though I had reached the same conclusion independently). . . ."[36]

On our very first day, we asked in our first interview with Ambassador Qian Dayong his impression and judgment of President Nixon.

As a careful student, he said, he 'would not make snap judgments' or 'one sentence comments' such as those blurbs 'often used to promote book sales.' Before we asked any more questions, Qian said "I would like to offer an over-all assessment."

"My assessment is that the primary duty of a president is to apply the laws that protect his country. Nixon made mighty contributions to fulfill that primary duty as Commander-in-Chief. That is why," he went on to say, "President Nixon is respected, admired, and loved, not only in China, but in the world." "He was," said Qian Dayong, "a great statesman but he was also a shrewd politician."

"One reason," explained Qian Dayong, "was that he recognized the limits of U.S. strengths."

As a master of geo-politics, Nixon realized that the Vietnam conflict had sapped American power. That was why his first decision as Chief Executive, said Qian, was to "de-Americanize the Vietnam war." He began U.S. troop withdrawals from Vietnam only a few months after he took office.

Ambassador Qian then alluded to Nixon's Kansas City speech where he realistically recognized the "five big powers," one of which was China. He knew that an accommodation with the People's Republic would force the Soviet Union into a defensive position, since the Soviets, believed Nixon, thought that the Vietnam conflict had put the U.S. to disadvantage. By opening relations with China, and withdrawing from Vietnam, Nixon then turned the tables on the Soviet Union, explained Ambassador Qian.

Dr. Milton Friedman, Nobel Laureate in Economics, once paid tribute to the brilliance of Nixon. He said of the five presidents he had advised, "Nixon had the highest I.Q." Former Secretary of State General Alexander Haig was of the opinion that "Richard Nixon was the best president of the last forty years."

Mme. Zhang Ying said it another way, "Nixon was a man with vision." She then went on to say that she had met with five presidents—Nixon, Ford, Carter, Reagan, and George H.W. Bush. The four who followed Nixon could not match "his intellect and knowledge of foreign policy". She then asked if we had read any of his books on foreign policy after he left the presidency. James Humes and Edward Nixon nodded, "Yes." They have been translated into Chinese. No one, without knowledge of history or his four decades of meeting with leaders around the world, could have written those books. Like Chou En-lai, Mr. Nixon was "a man of thought."

The then Deputy Foreign Minister for Foreign Affairs, Yang Jiechi, (by 2008, Yang Jiechi was Foreign Minister), a youngish man hardly looking forty, dressed in his blazer and gray flannels, told us at the Chinese Foreign Office the impression he gleaned from his predecessors was that Nixon was "the only president who overwhelmed them with his acumen and knowledge of foreign policy." He was including those Chinese leaders who had dined with Nixon in his Saddle River, New Jersey, home after he left office. "Presidents today," Yang Jiechi added, "don't have time to think and reflect." Nixon, however, allotted time in the White House, he understood, for that purpose. He went on to say that Nixon was a real leader who manifested contempt for those in politics who "shape policy to fit the latest polls."

Yang Jiechi then said—like others we met—that he had read Nixon's books and admired his "direct writing style." "He could," summed up Yang Jiechi, "express something profound in the simplest terms."

One knew, said Jiechi, that like Chou En-lai, Charles deGaulle, and Winston Churchill, Nixon was a "student of history."

As an example, he told us that he laughed when he read Nixon's line that "like Disraeli did, he had 'dished the Whigs,' meaning outflanking the Democrats on the left," such as going to China.

Ambassador Zhang Yijun, in his interview, paid tribute to Nixon's command of foreign policy. "Unlike any of the presidents, or for that matter any of the envoys or ambassadors to the People's Republic, I never saw him refer to notes or consult with aides." "He was," he added, "always prepared." In addition, Zhang Yijun added his personal impression of Nixon that might surprise readers. "He was the warmest and most approachable of any American leader we met." James Humes, who was a speech writer for five presidents (all the Republican presidents from Eisenhower to the first President Bush), also has this same opinion—that President Nixon was the most approachable and the easiest to talk to on questions of policy.

Ambassador Jiang Chengzong, who would serve as our tour guide on our trip, also provided these insights into Nixon's human side:

As they took him on that snowy trip to the Great Wall, Nixon told him the two things that he always wanted to do in his life were "to eat Peking Duck in Peking and visit the Great Wall." He also added that at a luncheon following the Great Wall and Ming Tombs trip, they offered him Western food which he declined saying, "No. Why would anyone eat American food in China?"

But it was the irrepressible 'Little Ji' who summed it all up with a chuckle. The teenage 'Truman Hater' now turned seventy year-old 'Nixon Admirer' said, "Only Nixon, a Republican president, could have pulled it off."

Our everyday guide, Ambassador Jiang Chengzong, also put in some good words for Mrs. Nixon: "From the moment Mrs. Nixon stepped off the American plane wearing that bright red dress, I had a feeling the trip was going to be a success. Red is a good omen for the Chinese."

He realized later that her choice of red was no accident. "She had done her homework, as you Americans say, just like her husband." She also wielded "chopsticks like she was raised on a rice paddy."

While the president was engaged in negotiations, she was taken to see selected sites. Ambassador Jiang Chengzong was an observer in many of her stop-bys and visits. When some of those who were showing her around spieled off Communist dogma—perhaps more to impress attending Party functionaries like Jiang Chengzong—she would graciously deflect their discourses saying "I have read Marx and Engels too." Her sincere interest in things Chinese and her winning charm was never more manifest than when "talking with children."

The scholarly Qian Dayong was, perhaps, the most intimately involved in preparations for the Nixon visit. This English-speaking specialist on American relations talked out plans with both Doctor Kissinger and later with General Haig. For the actual Nixon visit he was alongside both Chou En-lai and Mao in their historic discussions.

It was, as previously stated, a last minute decision for the ailing Mao to get out of his sick bed to greet the President. Qian Dayong stressed the importance of the first sentence the President said to Mao. It was not the small talk of amenities. Nixon, said Qian Dayong, knew exactly what would touch the right chord with Mao: "I come to China for our mutual interest." In other words, it was in the self-interest of both giant world powers to meet.

When Mao heard the translator deliver the words, he nodded and smiled.

On Air Force One to Beijing, President Nixon had earlier written out on a yellow legal pad notes to organize his thoughts and rehearse to himself his approach to Chairman Mao.

WHAT THEY WANT

1. Build up their world credentials
2. Taiwan
3. Get us out of Asia

WHAT WE WANT

1. Indo-China (?)
2. Communication—to restrain Chinese expansion in Asia
3. In future—Reduce threat of confrontation or conflict by China Super Power

WHAT WE BOTH WANT

1. Reduce danger of confrontation and conflict
2. A more stable Asia
3. A restraint on U.S.S.R.[37]

Nixon's first sentence to Chairman Mao reduced these points to a phrase "for our mutual interest."

Qian Dayong told us that as soon as he saw Mao's reaction to Nixon's opening words, he was confident there was going to be some kind of communiqué worked out despite the difficulties over Taiwan.

Mme. Zhang Ying recalled that President Nixon gave Chairman Mao a rock from the moon that the U.S. Astronauts had brought back, and Mao was pleased with the gift. She and her husband were later given a piece of it by Mao, which they treasure. Mme. Zhang Ying, a blunt woman not easily given to overstatement, told us "I knew at that time Nixon came that this was 'an historical event.'" But she said "It was much more than any of us imagined. Like the moon voyage itself, it was an epic making event of the centuries. It was monumental."

Ambassador Zhang Yijun, who worked in preparations at the time in the Foreign Office, echoed the same judgment this way: "It made history—but making it happen from the secret negotiations that lead to the open agreement was 'the most exciting drama of my life.'"

In our discussions with the learned Ambassador Qian Dayong that very first full day in Beijing on September 22, the words of Confucius came up in relation to the Nixon trip. It seems that at a young age the new Emperor of the Zhou Dynasty came to the throne in the fifth century B.C. The young man in his twenties turned to the imperial family's most trusted adviser and wisest philosopher and asked, "What is the most important advice you can give me in ruling the Middle Kingdom?"

And Confucius answered, "First you have to define the problem."

It was agreed that Nixon correctly 'defined' the problem confronting the United States that prevented any opening of their relations. That problem, concluded Nixon, was not the U.S. engagement in the conflict in Vietnam, nor the ideological gulf between Communism and democratic capitalism. The Taiwan issue defined the problem. The People's Republic saw it as their province. The United States viewed it as a separate nation with whom it had defense treaties.

This issue provoked the hottest disagreements in initial negotiations that took place in Beijing. It was Nixon who first figured a solution to the impasse. In his visits to Taiwan as Vice-President, he knew that it was a matter of faith to the Chinese Nationalists that Chiang Kai-shek would one day return as the head of China. The Red Chinese, Nixon realized, also believed that the province of Taiwan would eventually be theirs again. In other words, both the Nationalist and Red Chinese believed in a "One China."

Once that face-saving formula for both sides was devised to cover over the deep abyss of differences that separated the two countries, it should be possible. In the words of Lao-Tse, "A journey of a thousand miles begins with a single step."

Like the ancient sages from both the Biblical and Athenian times, the Chinese can boast of the earliest philosophers. Their gifts to civilization are immense. Anyone who visits China, even briefly, can begin to glimpse their wonders. Not the least of their contributions is cuisine. The Chinese published the first cook book and were preparing gourmet meals when the Gauls or the French were still cooking over campfires.

Ambassador Jiang Chengzong, at our last evening dinner in Shanghai, pointed to the cuisine in each of three successive places we visited that replicated the Nixon trip in 1972: Beijing, Hangzhou, and Shanghai.

President Nixon, he related, in one of his toasts in his last dinner in Shanghai mentioned the cuisines associated with each area. Spicy like the food in Chairman Mao's native Hunan in Beijing—a bit salty in the lake resort of Hangzhou—and then on the sweetish side in the food of Shanghai. In Beijing the hot problem of Taiwan had to be resolved. Then in Hangzhou, discussions now centering on the wording of the communiqué was not as hot as Beijing, but still spirited or salty. But here in Shanghai, after everything had been worked out, it was all "sweetness and light."

At the last banquet President Nixon concluded with the observation "We have been here a week. This was the week that changed the world."[38]

The world would change.

Gradually the success of the new course was evident. With the new rapprochement with the People's Republic, the Soviets believed they had to come to some accommodation with the U.S. In May, 1972, the U.S. and Russia signed the S.A.L.T. treaty, so for the first time two nations agreed to limits on nuclear weapons.[39]

The People's Republic's new acceptance of the capitalist America would eventually begin to encourage private business ventures after Mao's death in 1976. In 1998, a slogan on Beijing billboards read "To Get Rich is Glorious."[40]

In the Shanghai luncheon of our last day of our trip, we were hosted, as mentioned earlier, by a former mayor of Shanghai. He related how his predecessor in the 1970's, one of the "Gang of Four," did everything he could to block the Nixon trip. Then he said that he understood how from the American side there were influential forces, both in the government and non-governmental interest groups, which opposed the trip.

James Humes had been asked in 1969, by President Nixon, to help compose the words to be written on a plaque to be left at the site of the first moon landing. The plaque, mounted on the leg of the L.E.M. vehicle there, had the signatures of President Nixon as well as astronauts Aldrin, Armstrong, and Collins beneath it. The words were:

> Here men from the planet Earth
> first set foot upon the moon
> July, 1969 A.D.
> We came in Peace for all Mankind

The author brought photographs of the earth as seen from the moon signed by the three astronauts, and gave them to the former mayor.

The former mayor rose and toasted in his halting but deliberate words: "The two things I never thought would come to pass in my lifetime were men landing on the moon, and an American president coming to China. And of the two, the second was the most difficult."

NOTES

1. Tuchman, *Stilwell*, 311, 378, 379, 382, 511
2. Tuchman, *If Mao*, 77
3. Ibid., 77, 78, 79, 80, 82
4. Nixon, *RN*, 565
5. Ibid.
6. Chaozhu, 21
7. Ibid., 43
8. Ibid., 44, and personal communication
9. Ibid., 38, and personal communication
10. Ibid., 39
11. Ibid., 46
12. Ibid., 53
13. Ibid., 54
14. Ibid., 55
15. Ibid., 56
16. Ibid., 57
17. Ibid.
18. Ibid.
19. Ibid.
20. Ibid.
21. Ibid.
22. Ibid., xviii
23. Ibid., 58
24. Ibid.
25. Ibid.
26. Ibid., 59
27. Ibid., 330
28. Ibid., 259
29. Ibid., 262

30. Ibid., 194
31. Ibid., 141, 210
32. Kissinger, 740
33. Ibid., 741
34. Ibid.
35. Aitken, 362
36. Kissinger, 1086
37. Mann, 13, 14
38. videotape
39. videotape
40. videotape

Bibliography

Aitken, Jonathan. *Nixon: A Life*. Washington D.C.: Regnery Publishing, Inc., 1993.
American Press Corps. *The President's Trip to China*. New York: Bantam Books, 1972.
Becker, Jasper. *The Chinese*. 2000.
Chang, Jung. *Wild Swans*. New York: Simon & Schuster, 1991. First Touchstone Edition, 2003. (Pages and page numbers of the text are identical in both editions.)
Chang, Jung, and Jon Halliday. *Mao: The Unknown Story*. New York: Anchor Books—A division of Random House, 2006.
Chaozhu, Ji. *The Man on Mao's Right: From Harvard Yard to Tiananmen Square, My Life Inside China's Foreign Ministry*. New York: Random House, 2008.
de Gaulle, Charles. *The Edge of the Sword*, Faber & Faber, 1960.
Fairbank, John King, Merle Goldman. *China: A New History*. Cambridge, Massachusetts: Belknap Press, 1998.
Ford, Gerald R. *A Time to Heal*. New York: Harper & Row, 1979.
Greenstein, Fred. *The Hidden Hand Presidency*. Baltimore: The Johns Hopkins University Press, 1994.
Haldeman, H.R. *The Haldeman Diaries*. New York: G.P. Putnam's Sons, 1994.
Humes, James C. *Nixon's Ten Commandments of Statecraft*. New York: Scribner, 1997.
Kissinger, Henry. *White House Years*. Boston: Little, Brown and Company, 1979.
Mann, James. *About Face*. New York: Vintage Books—a division of Random House, 2000.
Nixon, Richard. *Foreign Affairs,* October, 1967.
———. *Leaders*. New York: Warner Books, 1982.
———. *RN: The Memoirs of Richard Nixon*. New York: Simon & Schuster, 1990.
Nixon's China Game, "The American Experience", PBS Home Video (videotape), 2000, WGBH Educational Foundation. Running time: approximately 60 min. (Endnotes for this reference will be noted "videotape".)

Tuchman, Barbara W. *"If Mao Had Come to Washington in 1945: an essay in Alternatives,"* Foreign Affairs, October, 1972. Reprinted by permission in *Notes From China*. New York: Macmillan Publishing Company, U.S.A., 1972.

———. *Stilwell and the American Experience in China, 1911-45*. New York: Grove Press, 1971.

Wenqian, Gao. *Zhou Enlai: The Last Perfect Revolutionary*. New York: PublicAffairs, 2007.

Index

Photos are indicated by p1, p2, etc. The photo section follows page 32.

ABMs. *See* Anti-Ballistic Missiles
Acheson, Dean, 9, 41
Adams, Sherman, 9
Agnew, Spiro, 43, 46
Aitken, Jonathan, 29, 50
Albania, 15
"America the Beautiful," 5
Anti-Ballistic Missiles (ABMs), 43
Arbatov, Georgi, 48
"Asia After Vietnam" (Nixon, R.), 64
Atlee, Clement, 30

Badaling, p25–p28
Becker, Jaspar, 34
Beijing, 35, p1–p24
Benson, Ezra Taft, 9
Brezhnev, Leonid, 29, 35
Britain, 30
Brown, Pat, 8, 24
Buck, Pearl, 55
Bush, George H.W., 27, 65

California, 23, 24, p37
Castro, Fidel, 8, 35
Ceausceu, Nicolae, 44, 45
chess, 4
Chiang Ching, 5, 16, 17, 38

Chiang Kai-shek, 3, 20, 40; Nixon, R., and, 7–8, 51, 69; purges of, 18; U.S. and, 54, 55, 58
Chicago Bulls, p9
China: culture of, 70; deGaulle on, 25; diplomacy of, 3, 4, 5, 6, 21, 35, 41–42, 54–55, 56; Great Wall of, 4, 67, p25–p28; industrialization of, 13–14, 34; Kissinger in, 47–48; medicine in, 19; military of, 4–5, 16, 17, 34–35, 37; *New York Times* on, 15; Nixon, R., and, 5, 7–8, 12, 21, 23, 25, 30, 40, 44–45, 46–47, 48–49, 50–52, 56, 60, 64–66, 68, 70–71; starvation in, 15–16; steel in, 14, 15–16, 34; in U.N., 65; U.S. and, 41–42, 43, 54–56, 58; U.S.S.R. and, 13, 14–15, 16, 34–35, 39, 40, 43, 57. *See also* Cultural Revolution; Mao Tse-tung
China: A New History (Fairbank and Goldman), 18
China World Hotel, p5–7, p22
Chinese (Becker), 34
Chinese People's Institute of Foreign Affairs (CPIFA), 3
Chou En-lai, 3, 4; biography of, 39; during Cultural Revolution, 6, 20;

Gang of Four and, 5, 62; Ji Chaozhu on, 61, 62; Kissinger and, 48, 60, 64, 65; Malraux on, 50; Nixon, R., and, 45, 51–52, 59–60, 63, p14
Churchill, Winston, 38, 49, 67
Churchill, Winston, II, 1, 49–50, p36
Cold War, 24
collectivization, 15
Colorado, p36
Confucius, 55, 69
Conscience of a Conservative (Goldwater), 24
Council on Foreign Relations, 55
Cover Your Ass. *See* C.Y.A.
CPIFA. *See* Chinese People's Institute of Foreign Affairs
Cuba, 11
Cultural Revolution, 17, 19, 59; Chou En-lai during, 6, 20; classless society in, 5, 18, 33; deaths in, 23; Jiang Chengzong during, 21; P.L.A. in, 37; Tang Longbin during, 21
C.Y.A. (Cover Your Ass), 41

Dai Hong (Tracy), p32
deGaulle, Charles, 24–25, 50
Demilitarized Zone, 31
Deng Xiaoping, 16, 64
détente, 25
Dewey, Thomas E., 41
Diaoyutal State Guest House, p1–p4
The Diplomatic History of Sino-U.S. Relations (Wang Li), 60, 65
Dixon, George, 7
doctors, 19
Douglas, Helen Gahagan, 11
DreiHussaren Hotel, 36
Dulles, John Foster, 9, 10, 41, 51, 56

The Edge of the Sword (deGaulle), 25
Eisenhower, Dwight, 7; Nixon, R., under, 8–9, 11; on Rockefeller, 23
Eisenhower, Julie Nixon, p38
Ellsworth, Robert, 30
Environmental Protection Agency, 47

Evans, Tom, 28, 30–31

Fairbank, John King, 18
Federal Family Assistance, 47
Finch, Bob, 24, 27
"Five Powers of Influence" (Nixon, R.), 60, 64, 66
Forbidden City, p24
Ford, Gerald, p37
Foreign Affairs, 23, 30, 55
Foreign Policy Luncheon, 2
Formosa, 7, 41, 44, 58, 69. *See also* Chiang Kai-shek
Friedman, Milton, 66

Gang of Four, 5, 6, 38, 40, 49, 62, 70. *See also* Chiang Ching
Gao Wenqian, 39
Geneva Convention, 51, 56, 59
going native, 40–41
Goldman, Merle, 18
Goldwater, Barry, 24, 26, 27, 28
Great Hall of the People, p13
The Great Leap Forward, 13–16, 59
Great Wall of China, 4, 67, p25–p28
Greenstein, Fred, 9
Guam Doctrine, 31
Guo Jiading, 51, 62, p11

Haig, Alexander, 5–6, 43, 49, 66
Haldeman, H.R., 46
handshake, 51–52, p14
Hangzhou, 3, p30–p33; Haig's trip in, 5–6; Mao's retreat to, 16, p30
Hartman, Arthur, 65
Herter Report, 11
The Hidden Hand Presidency (Greenstein), 9
Hiss, Alger, 10, 23
Hitler, Adolph, 38
Ho Chi Minh, 8, 36
Home, Alexander Douglas-, 24, 29–30
Humes, Dianne Stuart, 2, 4; pictures of, p1–p4, p6, p11–p13, p16–p22, p24–p26, p31–p32, p36, p38

Humes, James C., 2; on Hiss, 10; *Nixon's Ten Commandments of Statecraft* by, x, 1, 49; pictures of, p1–p4, p6, p11–p13, p15–p22, p24–p26, p31–p32, p36–p38; Scranton and, 26–27
Humes, John P., 36
Humphrey, George, 9
Hurley, Pat, 54, 55

"If Mao Had Come to Washington in 1945: An Essay in Alternatives" (Tuchman), 55
Indonesia, 35
Israel, 40

Jiang Chengzong: during Cultural Revolution, 21; at Great Wall, 4, 67; photo-ops with, 3–4; pictures of, p1–p3, p11–p13, p16–p22, p24–p25, p31
Ji Chaozhu, 56–57, p14–p15; on Chou En-lai, 61, 62; *The Man on Mao's Right* by, 19, 58–59
Johnson, Lyndon (LBJ), 26; Nixon, R., and, 28; Rusk and, 42; on Vietnam, 31
Jung Chang, 15, 20, 21

Kazakhstan, 34–35
Kennedy, Jacqueline, 26
Kennedy, Joe, 10
Kennedy, John, 10, 11–12, 26
Kennedy, Robert, 10, 31
Khan, Yahya, 45, 46
Khrushchev, Nikita, 13, 16
Kissinger, Henry, 40; in China, 47–48; Chou En-lai and, 48, 60, 64, 65; Nixon, R., and, 42–43, 46–47, 65
Knowland, William, 8
Kramer, Fritz, 47
Kremlin, 13

Landon, Alf, 28
Lao-Tse, 70

Latin America, 29, 35–36
LBJ. *See* Johnson, Lyndon
Leaders (Nixon, R.), 45, 51
Lerner, Max, 48
lightning rods, 9
Li-Kwan-Chou, 54
Lin Biao, 16, 36–38, 49
Little Red Book, 17, 19, 37
Liu Shaoqi, 16, 17
Lloyd, Selwyn, 29
Long March, 16
Louis, Victor, 35

MacMillan, Harold, 48, 49
Madame Mao. *See* Chiang Ching
Malraux, Andre, 50
The Man on Mao's Right (Ji Chaozhu), 19, 58–59
Mao Tse-tung, 3, 13–14; Anti-Rightist campaign of, 17, 18; comeback of, 16–17; Hangzhou retreat by, 16, p30; Malraux on, 50; Nixon, R., and, 39, 51, 62, 68–69; U.S. and, 38–39, 42, 55; Vietnam and, 36, 42
Mao Yuanxin, 19
McCarthy, Joe, 10, 58
McWhorter, Charles K., 28
"Meet the Press," 29
Mikoyan, Anastas, 9–10
Miller, Bill, 27
Ming Tombs, 4, p29
Molotov-Ribbentrop pact, 38
moon landing, 69, 70–71
Murphy, Happy, 27

National Security Council, 42, 43
New China Agency, 59
New York Times: on China, 15; on Nixon, R., 10, 11, 29, 42
Nixon, Edward, 1, 2; pictures of, p1–p4, p6, p11–p13, p15–p17, p19–p22, p24–p27, p29, p31, p34–p35
Nixon, Mudge, Stern, Baldwin, and Todd, 24
Nixon, Pat, 3, 24, 63, 67–68

Nixon, Richard: Chiang Kai-shek and, 7–8, 51, 69; China and, 5, 7–8, 12, 21, 23, 25, 30, 40, 44–45, 46–47, 48–49, 50–52, 56, 60, 64–66, 68, 70–71; Chou En-lai and, 45, 51–52, 59–60, 63, p14; deGaulle and, 24–25, 50; under Eisenhower, 8–9, 11; European trips of, 24, 29; "Five Powers of Influence" speech by, 60, 64, 66; for *Foreign Affairs*, 23, 30; Foreign Policy Statement of, 45; gubernatorial campaign of, 23–24; handshake by, 51–52, p14; as icon, ix–x, 2, 66, 67; Johnson and, 28; on Kennedy, John, 11–12, 26; Kissinger and, 42–43, 46–47, 65; Mao Tse-tung and, 39, 51, 62, 68–69; *New York Times* on, 10, 11, 29, 42; picture of, p14; silent majority speech by, 19; Tang Longbin and, 63–64; tree planting by, 3, p32–p33; U.S. Department of State under, 41; U.S.S.R. and, 9–10, 24, 50; Vietnam and, 28, 31, 64
Nixon's China Game, 38–39
Nixon's Ten Commandments of Statecraft (Humes, James), x, 1, 49
nuclear shelters, 35

1000 Cadre Conference, 16
Organization of American States, 11
Ottawa, Canada, 6

panda bears, 63
Peng Zhen, 16, 17
Pennsylvania, p38
People's Liberation Army (P.L.A.), 17, 37
phone call, 4–5
photo-ops, 3–4
Ping-Pong, 45–46
P.L.A. *See* People's Liberation Army
Presidential Palace, 5
The President's Trip to China, 59

press corps, 5
Price, Ray, 30

Qian Dayong, 64, 65–66, 68, 69, p12
Qinghua University, 17
Quayle, Dan, 3
Quemoy-Matsu Islands, 11

Rayburn, Sam, 26
Reagan, Ronald, 31
Rebozo, Bebe, 26
Red Army, 4–5, 16
Red Fir tree, 3, p32–p33
Red Guards, 17
Republican Party, 8–9
Reston, James, 29
Rhyne, Charles, 49
Rockefeller, Nelson, 23, 26, 27
Rogers, William, 10, 41, 42
Romania, 15, 45
Roosevelt, Franklin D., 55
Rusk, Dean, 42
Ryals, Jarvis D., 1, 30; pictures of, p1–p4, p11–p13, p15–p22, p24–p26, p31, p36–p38

Sacred Way, p29
Salisbury, Harrison, 64
S.A.L.T. *See* Strategic Arms Limitation Treaty
Schell, Joe, 24
Scranton, William, 26–27
Service, John, 40
Shanghai, 6, 70, p34–p35
Six Crises (Nixon, R.), 23
Smathers, George, 26
Smith, Walter Bedell, 56
Snow, Edgar, 44
snowfall, 4
Sorensen, Ted, 12
South Korea, 9
Stalin, Joseph, 13, 14, 38
steel, 14, 15–16, 34
Stevenson, Adlai, 23–24, 25, 41

Stilwell, Joseph, 54
Stoessel, Walter, 41
Strategic Arms Limitation Treaty (S.A.L.T.), 36, 65, 70
Sun-Yat-Sen, 3, 4

Taft, Robert, 8
Taiwan, 7, 41, 44, 58, 69. *See also* Chiang Kai-shek
Tang, Nancy, 64
Tang Longbin, 3, p21; during Cultural Revolution, 21; at Ming Tombs, 4; Nixon, R., and, 63–64
Tang RongRong, p1, p2
Thieu, Nguyen Van, 31
Third World Conference, 35
Thirty Seconds Over Tokyo, 57
Thomas, Helen, 4–5
Thurmond, Strom, 31
Tiananmen Square, p23
TIME, 44
Truman, Harry, 11, 40
Tuchman, Barbara, 55

U.N. *See* United Nations
United Nations (U.N.), 65
United States (U.S.): Chiang Kai-shek and, 54, 55, 58; China and, 41–42, 43, 54–56, 58; Mao Tse-tung and, 38–39, 42, 55; State Department, 2, 40–41; U.S.S.R. and, 13, 14–15, 16, 34–35, 39, 40, 43, 57, 70; Vietnam and, 43

U.S.S.R.: China and, 13, 14–15, 16, 34–35, 39, 40, 43, 57; history of, 10–11; Nixon, R., and, 9–11, 24, 50; U.S. and, 13, 14–15, 16, 34–35, 39, 40, 43, 57, 70; Verona files of, 10

Venezuela, 9
Vice-Presidency, 8
Vicker's Tavern, p38
Vietnam: Johnson on, 31; Mao Tse-tung and, 36, 42; Nixon, R., and, 28, 31, 64; U.S. and, 43

Wallace, George, 19
Wang Li, 41, 60, 65, p16
Wedgwood, John, 35
Wei Jingsheng, 15
Weinstein, Allen, 10
White House Years (Kissinger), 65
Wikipedia, 49
Wild Swans (Jung Chang), 15
Woods, Rosemary, 30

Yang Jiechi, 66–67, p19
Young Republicans, 28

Zhang Hanzhi, 38–39, 49
Zhang Yijun, 6, 54, 55, 60, 67, 69, p18
Zhang Ying, 21, 66, 69, p22
Zhou Enlai: The Last Perfect Revolutionary (Gao Wenqian), 39
Zi Zhongyun, 60–61, 62, p17

www.ingramcontent.com/pod-product-compliance
Lightning Source LLC
Chambersburg PA
CBHW021131300426
44113CB00006B/375